Famous authors tell you about their

Beautiful, loving and nutty

Dogs

Famous authors tell you about their

Beautiful, loving and nutty Dogs

JANE ROCKWELL

A BULL'S-EYE BOOK

Published by
William Mulvey Inc.
72 Park Street
New Canaan, Conn. 06840

Cover design: Louis Kelley
Interior design: Angela Foote

Library of Congress Cataloging-in-Publication Data

Famous authors tell you about their
Beautiful, loving and nutty
Dogs
"A Bull's-eye Book"

1. Dogs—Literary collections.   2. American literature.   3. English literature.   4. Dogs—Anecdotes.
I. Rockwell, Jane.

PS509.D6F36   1988   810'8'036   88–42811

ISBN 0–934791–17–1

Printed in the United States of America
First Edition

Cover photo © 1981 by Hallmark
Cards, Inc., Kansas City, Missouri.

Staunch & faithful little lovers that they are, they give back a hundred fold every sign of love one ever gives them—& it mitigates the pang of losing them to know how very happy a little affection has made them.

Edith Wharton

Contents

Contents

Gulliver the Great

WALTER A. DYER

It was a mild evening in early spring, and the magnolias were in bloom. We motored around the park, turned up a side street, and finally came to a throbbing standstill before the Churchwarden Club.

There was nothing about its exterior to indicate that it was a clubhouse at all, but within there was an indefinable atmosphere of early Victorian comfort. There was something about it that suggested Mr. Pickwick. Old prints of horses and ships and battles hung upon the walls, and the oak was dark and old. There seemed to be no decorative scheme or keynote, and yet the atmosphere was utterly distinctive. It was my first visit to the Churchwarden Club, of which my quaint, old-fashioned Uncle Ford had long been a member, and I was charmed.

We dined in the rathskeller, the walls of which were completely covered with long churchwarden pipes, arranged in the most intricate and marvelous patterns; and after our mutton-chop and ale and plum pudding, we filled with the choicest of tobaccos the pipes which the old major-domo brought us.

Then came Jacob R. Enderby to smoke with us.

Tall and spare he was, with long, straight, black hair, large, aquiline nose, and piercing eyes. I disgraced myself by staring at him. I didn't know such a man existed in New York, and yet I couldn't decide whether his habitat should be Arizona or Cape Cod.

Enderby and Uncle Ford were deep in a discussion of the statesmanship of James G. Blaine, when a waiter summoned my uncle to the telephone.

1

I neglected to state that my uncle, in his prosaic hours, is a physician; and this was a call. I knew it the moment I saw the waiter approaching. I was disappointed and disgusted.

Uncle Ford saw this and laughed.

"Cheer up!" said he. "You needn't come with me to visit the sick. I'll be back in an hour, and meanwhile Mr. Enderby will take care of you; won't you, Jake?"

For answer Enderby arose, and refilling his pipe took me by the arm, while my uncle got into his overcoat. As he passed us on the way out he whispered in my ear:

"Talk about dogs."

I heard and nodded.

Enderby led me to the lounge or loafing-room, an oak-paneled apartment in the rear of the floor above, with huge leather chairs and a seat in the bay window. Save for a gray-haired old chap dozing over a copy of *Simplicissimus,* the room was deserted.

But no sooner had Enderby seated himself on the window-seat than there was a rush and a commotion, and a short, glad bark, and Nubbins, the steward's bull-terrier, bounded in and landed at Enderby's side with canine expressions of great joy.

I reached forward to pat him, but he paid absolutely no attention to me.

At last his wrigglings subsided, and he settled down with his head on Enderby's knee, the picture of content. Then I recalled my Uncle's parting injunction.

"Friend of yours?" I suggested.

Enderby smiled. "Yes," he said, "we're friends, I guess. And the funny part of it is that he doesn't pay any attention to any one else except his master. They all act that way with me, dogs do." And he pulled Nubbins's stubby ears.

"Natural attraction, I suppose," said I.

"Yes, it is," he answered, with the modest frankness of a big man. "It's a thing hard to explain, though there's a sort of reason for it in my case."

I pushed toward him a little tobacco-laden teak-wood stand hopefully. He refilled and lighted.

"It's an extraordinary thing, even so," he said, puffing. "Every dog nowadays seems to look upon me as his long-lost master; but it wasn't always so. I hated dogs and they hated me."

Not wishing to say "Really" or "Indeed" to this big, outdoor man, I simply grunted my surprise.

"Yes, we were born enemies. More than that, I was afraid of dogs. A little fuzzy toy dog, ambling up to me in a room full of company, with his tail wagging, gave me the shudders. I couldn't touch the beast. And as for big dogs outdoors, I feared them like the plague. I would go blocks out of my way to avoid one.

"I don't remember being particularly cowardly about other things, but I just couldn't help this. It was in my blood, for some reason or other. It was the bane of my existence. I couldn't see what the brutes were put in the world for, or how any one could have anything to do with them.

"All the dogs reciprocated. They disliked and distrusted me. The most docile old Brunos would growl and show their teeth when I came near."

"Did the change come suddenly?" I asked.

"Quite. It was in 1901. I accepted a commission from an importing and trading company to go to the Philippines to do a little quiet exploring, and spent four months in the sickly place. Then I got the fever, and when I recovered I couldn't get out of there too soon.

"I reached Manila just in time to see the mail steamer disappearing around the point, and I was mad. There would be another in six days, but I couldn't wait. I was just crazy to get back home.

"I made inquiries and learned of an old tramp steamer, named the *Old Squaw*, making ready to leave for Honolulu on the following day with a cargo of hemp and stuff, and a bunch of Moros for some show in the States, and I booked passage on that.

"She was the worst old tub you ever saw. I didn't learn much about her, but I verily believe her to have been a condemned excursion boat. She wouldn't have been allowed to run to Coney Island.

"She was battered and unpainted, and she wallowed horribly. I don't believe she could have reached Honolulu much before the regular boat, but I couldn't wait, and I took her.

"I made myself as comfortable as possible, bribed the cook to insure myself against starvation, and swung a hammock on the forward deck as far as possible from the worst of the vile smells.

"But we hadn't lost sight of Manila Bay when I discovered that there was a dog aboard—and such a dog! I had never seen one that sent me into such a panic as this one, and he had free range of the ship. A Great Dane he was, named Gulliver, and he was the pride of the captain's rum-soaked heart.

"With all my fear, I realized he was a magnificent animal, but I looked on him as a gigantic devil. Without exception, he was the biggest dog I ever saw, and as muscular as a lion. He lacked some points that show judges set store by, but he had the size and the build.

"I had seen Vohl's Vulcan and the Württemberg breed, but they were fox-terriers compared with Gulliver. His tail was as big around as my arm, and the cook lived in terror of his getting into the galley and wagging it; and he had a mouth that looked to me like the crater of Mauna Loa, and a voice that shook the planking when he spoke.

"I first caught sight of him appearing from behind a huge coil of cordage in the stern. He stretched and yawned, and I nearly died of fright.

"I caught up a belaying-pin, though little good that would have done me. I think he saw me do it, and doubtless he set me down for an enemy then and there.

"We were well out of the harbor, and there was no turning back, but I would have given my right hand to be off that boat. I fully expected him to eat me up, and I slept with that belaying-pin sticking into my ribs in the hammock, and with my revolver loaded and handy.

"Fortunately, Gulliver's dislike for me took the form of sublime contempt. He knew I was afraid of him, and he despised me for it. He was a great pet with the captain and crew, and even the Moros treated him with admiring respect when they were allowed on deck. I couldn't understand it. I would as soon have made a pet of a hungry boa-constrictor.

"On the third day out the poor old boiler burst and the *Old*

Squaw caught fire. She was dry and rotten inside and she burned like tinder. No attempt was made to extinguish the flames, which got into the hemp in the hold in short order.

"The smoke was stifling, and in a jiffy all hands were struggling with the boats. The Moros came tumbling up from below and added to the confusion with their terrified yells.

"The davits were old and rusty, and the men were soon fighting among themselves. One boat dropped stern foremost, filled, and sank immediately, and the *Old Squaw* herself was visibly settling.

"I saw there was no chance of getting away in the boats, and I recalled a life-raft on the deck forward near my hammock. It was a sort of catamaran—a double platform on a pair of hollow, water-tight, cylindrical buoys. It wasn't twenty feet long and about half as broad, but it would have to do. I fancy it was a forgotten relic of the old excursion-boat days.

"There was no time to lose, for the *Old Squaw* was bound to sink presently. Besides, I was aft with the rest, and the flames were licking up the deck and running-gear in the waist of the boat.

"The galley, which was amidships near the engine-room, had received the full force of the explosion, and the cook lay moaning in the lee scuppers with a small water-cask thumping against his chest. I couldn't stop to help the man, but I did kick the cask away.

"It seemed to be nearly full, and it occurred to me that I should need it. I glanced quickly around, and luckily found a tin of biscuits that had also been blown out of the galley. I picked this up, and rolling the cask of water ahead of me as rapidly as I could, I made my way through the hot, stifling smoke to the bow of the boat.

"I kicked at the life-raft; it seemed to be sound, and I lashed the biscuits and water to it. I also threw on a coil of rope and a piece of sail-cloth. I saw nothing else about that could possibly be of any value to me. I abandoned my trunk for fear it would only prove troublesome.

"Then I hacked the raft loose with my knife and shoved it over the bulwark. Apparently no one had seen me, for there was no one else forward of the sheet of flame that now cut the boat in two.

"The raft was a mighty heavy affair, but I managed to raise one end to the rail. I don't believe I would ever have been able to heave it over under any circumstances, but I didn't have to.

"I felt a great upheaval, and the prow of the *Old Squaw* went up into the air. I grabbed the ropes that I had lashed the food on with and clung to the raft. The deck became almost perpendicular, and it was a miracle that the raft didn't slide down with me into the flames. Somehow it stuck where it was.

"Then the boat sank with a great roar, and for about a thousand years, it seemed to me, I was under water. I didn't do anything, I couldn't think.

"I was only conscious of a tremendous weight of water and a feeling that I would burst open. Instinct alone made me cling to the raft.

"When it finally brought me to the surface I was as nearly dead as I care to be. I lay there on the thing in a half-conscious condition for an endless time. If my life had depended on my doing something, I would have been lost.

"Then gradually I came to, and began to spit out salt water and gasp for breath. I gathered my wits together and sat up. My hands were absolutely numb, and I had to loosen the grip of my fingers with the help of my toes. Odd sensation.

"Then I looked about me. My biscuits and water and rope were safe, but the sail-cloth had vanished. I remember that this annoyed me hugely at the time, though I don't know what earthly good it would have been.

"The sea was fairly calm, and I could see all about. Not a human being was visible, only a few floating bits of wreckage. Every man on board must have gone down with the ship and drowned, except myself.

"Then I caught sight of something that made my heart stand still. The huge head of Gulliver was coming rapidly toward me through the water!

"The dog was swimming strongly, and must have leaped from

the *Old Squaw* before she sank. My raft was the only thing afloat large enough to hold him, and he knew it.

"I drew my revolver, but it was soaking wet and useless. Then I sat down on the cracker tin and gritted my teeth and waited. I had been alarmed, I must admit, when the boiler blew up and the panic began, but that was nothing to the terror that seized me now.

"Here I was all alone on the top of the Pacific Ocean with a horrible demon making for me as fast as he could swim. My mind was benumbed, and I could think of nothing to do. I trembled and my teeth rattled. I prayed for a shark, but no shark came.

"Soon Gulliver reached the raft and placed one of his forepaws on it and then the other. The top of it stood six or eight inches above the water, and it took a great effort for the dog to raise himself. I wanted to kick him back, but I didn't dare to move.

"Gulliver struggled mightily. Again and again he reared his great shoulders above the sea, only to be cast back, scratching and kicking, at a lurch of the raft.

"Finally a wave favored him, and he caught the edge of the under platform with one of his hind feet. With a stupendous effort he heaved his huge bulk over the edge and lay sprawling at my feet, panting and trembling."

Enderby paused and gazed out of the window with a big sigh, as though the recital of his story had brought back some of the horror of his remarkable experience.

Nubbins looked up inquiringly, and then snuggled closer to his friend, while Enderby smoothed the white head.

"Well," he continued, "there we were. You can't possibly imagine how I felt unless you, too, have been afflicted with dog-fear. It was awful. And I hated the brute so. I could have torn him limb from limb if I had had the strength. But he was vastly more powerful than I. I could only fear him.

"By and by he got up and shook himself. I cowered on my cracker-tin, but he only looked at me contemptuously, went to the other end of the raft, and lay down to wait patiently for deliverance.

"We remained this way until nightfall. The sea was comparatively calm, and we seemed to be drifting but slowly. We were in the path of ships likely to be passing one way or the other, and I would have been hopeful of the outcome if it had not been for my feared and hated companion.

"I began to feel faint, and opened the cracker-tin. The biscuits were wet with salt water, but I ate a couple, and left the tin open to dry them. Gulliver looked around, and I shut the tin hastily. But the dog never moved. He was not disposed to ask any favors. By kicking the sides of the cask and prying with my knife, I managed to get the bung out and took a drink. Then I settled myself on the raft with my back against the cask, and longed for a smoke.

"The gentle motion of the raft produced a lulling effect on my exhausted nerves, and I began to nod, only to awake with a start, with fear gripping at my heart. I dared not sleep. I don't know what I thought Gulliver would do to me, for I did not understand dogs, but I felt that I must watch him constantly. In the starlight I could see that his eyes were open. Gulliver was watchful too.

"All night long I kept up a running fight with drowsiness. I dozed at intervals, but never for long at a time. It was a horrible night, and I cannot tell you how I longed for day and welcomed it when it came.

"I must have slept toward dawn, for I suddenly became conscious of broad daylight. I roused myself, stood up, and swung my arms and legs to stir up circulation, for the night had been chilly. Gulliver arose, too, and stood silently watching me until I ceased for fear. When he had settled down again I got my breakfast out of the cracker-tin. Gulliver was restless, and was evidently interested.

" 'He must be hungry,' I thought, and then a new fear caught me. I had only to wait until he became very hungry and then he would surely attack me. I concluded that it would be wiser to feed him, and I tossed him a biscuit.

"I expected to see him grab it ravenously, and wondered as soon as I had thrown it if the taste of food would only serve to make him more ferocious. But at first he would not touch it. He only lay there with his great head on his paws and glowered at me. Distrust was plainly visible in his face. I had never realized before that a dog's face could express the subtler emotions.

"His gaze fascinated me, and I could not take my eyes from his. The bulk of him was tremendous as he lay there, and I noticed the big, swelling muscles of his jaw. At last he arose, sniffed suspiciously at the biscuit, and looked up at me again.

" 'It's all right; eat it!' I cried.

"The sound of my own voice frightened me. I had not intended to speak to him. But in spite of my strained tone he seemed somewhat reassured.

"He took a little nibble, and then swallowed the biscuit after one or two crunches, and looked up expectantly. I threw him another and he ate that.

" 'That's all,' said I, 'We must be sparing of them.'

"I was amazed to discover how perfectly he understood. He lay down again and licked his chops.

"Late in the afternoon I saw a line of smoke on the horizon, and soon a steamer hove into view. I stood up and waved my coat frantically, but to no purpose. Gulliver stood up and looked from me to the steamer, apparently much interested.

" 'Too far off,' I said to Gulliver. 'I hope the next one will come nearer.'

"At midday I dined, and fed Gulliver. This time he took the two biscuits quite without reserve and whacked his great tail against the raft. It seemed to me that his attitude was less hostile, and I wondered at it.

"When I took my drink from the cask, Gulliver showed signs of interest.

" 'I suppose dogs get thirsty, too,' I said aloud.

"Gulliver rapped with his tail. I looked about for some sort of receptacle, and finally pulled off my shoe, filled it with water, and shoved it toward him with my foot. He drank gratefully.

"During the afternoon I sighted another ship, but it was too distant to notice me. However, the sea remained calm and I did not despair.

"After we had had supper, I settled back against my cask, resolved to keep awake, for still I did not trust Gulliver. The sun set suddenly and the stars came out, and I found myself strangely lonesome. It seemed as though I had been alone out there on the Pacific for weeks. The miles and miles of heaving waters, almost on a level with my eye, were beginning to get on my nerves. I longed for someone to talk to, and wished I had dragged the half-breed cook along with me for company. I sighed loudly, and Gulliver raised his head.

" 'Lonesome out here, isn't it?' I said, simply to hear the sound of my own voice.

"Then for the first time Gulliver spoke. He made a deep sound in his throat, but it wasn't a growl, and with all my ignorance of dog language I knew it.

"Then I began to talk. I talked about everything—the people back home and all that—and Gulliver listened. I know more about dogs now, and I know that the best way to make friends with a dog is to talk to him. He can't talk back, but he can understand a heap more than you think he can.

"Finally Gulliver, who had kept his distance all this time, arose and came toward me. My words died in my throat. What was he going to do? To my immense relief he did nothing but sink down at my feet with a grunt and curl his huge body into a semicircle. He had dignity, Gulliver had. He wanted to be friendly, but he would not presume. However, I had lost interest in conversation, and sat watching him and wondering.

"In spite of my firm resolution, I fell asleep at length from sheer exhaustion, and never woke until daybreak. The sky was clouded and our raft was pitching. Gulliver was standing in the middle of the raft, looking at me in evident alarm. I glanced over my shoulder, and the blackness of the horizon told me that a storm was coming, and coming soon.

"I made fast our slender provender, tied the end of a line about my own waist for safety, and waited.

"In a short time the storm struck us in all its tropical fury. The raft pitched and tossed, now high up at one end, and now at the other, and sometimes almost engulfed in the waves.

"Gulliver was having a desperate time to keep aboard. His blunt claws slipped on the wet deck of the raft, and he fell and slid about dangerously. The thought flashed across my mind that the storm might prove to be a blessing in disguise, and that I might soon be rid of the brute.

"As I clung there to the lashings, I saw him slip down to the further end of the raft, his hind quarters actually over the edge. A wave swept over him, but still he clung, panting madly. Then the raft righted itself for a moment, and as he hung there he gave me a look I shall never forget—a look of fear, of pleading, of reproach, and yet of silent courage. And with all my stupidity I read that look. Somehow it told me that I was the master, after all, and he the dog. I could not resist it. Cautiously I raised myself and loosened the spare rope I had saved. As the raft tipped the other way Gulliver regained his footing and came sliding toward me.

"Quickly I passed the rope around his body, and as the raft dived again I hung on to the rope with one hand, retaining my own hold with the other. Gulliver's great weight nearly pulled my arm from its socket, but he helped mightily, and during the next moment of equilibrium I took another turn about his body and made the end of the rope fast.

"The storm passed as swiftly as it had come, and though it left us drenched and exhausted, we were both safe.

"That evening Gulliver crept close to me as I talked, and I let him. Loneliness will make a man do strange things.

"On the fifth day, when our provisions were nearly gone, and I had begun to feel the sinking dullness of despair, I sighted a steamer apparently coming directly toward us. Instantly I felt new life in my limbs and around my heart, and while the boat was yet miles away I began to shout and to wave my coat.

" 'I believe she's coming, old man!' I cried to Gulliver. 'I believe she's coming!'

"I soon wearied of this foolishness and sat down to wait. Gulliver came close and sat beside me, and for the first time I put my hand on him. He looked up at me and rapped furiously with his tail. I patted his head—a little gingerly, I must confess.

"It was a big, smooth head, and it felt solid and strong. I passed my hand down his neck, his back, his flanks. He seemed to quiver with joy. He leaned his huge body against me. Then he bowed his head and licked my shoe.

"A feeling of intense shame and unworthiness came over me, with the realization of how completely I had misunderstood him. Why should this great, powerful creature lick my shoe? It was incredible.

"Then, somehow, everything changed. Fear and distrust left me, and a feeling of comradeship and understanding took their place. We two had been through so much together. A dog was no longer a frightful beast to me; he was a dog! I cannot think of a nobler word. And Gulliver had licked my shoe! Doubtless it was only the fineness of his perception that had prevented him from licking my hand. I might have resented that. I put my arms suddenly around Gulliver's neck and hugged him, I loved that dog!

"Slowly, slowly, the steamer crawled along, but still kept to her course. When she was about a mile away, however, I saw that she would not pass as close to us as I had hoped; so I began once more my waving and yelling. She came nearer, nearer, but still showed no sign of observing us.

"She was abreast of us, and passing. I was in a frenzy!

"She was so near that I could make out the figure of the captain on the bridge, and other figures on the deck below. It seemed as though they must see us, though I realized how low in the water we stood, and how pitifully weak and hoarse my voice was. I had been a fool to waste it. Then an idea struck me.

" 'Speak!' I cried to Gulliver, who stood watching beside me. 'Speak, old man!'

"Gulliver needed no second bidding. A roar like that of all the bulls of Bashan rolled out over the blue Pacific. Again and again Gulliver gave voice, deep, full, powerful. His great side heaved with the mighty effort, his red, cavernous mouth open, and his head raised high.

" 'Good, old man!' I cried. 'Good!' And again that magnificent voice boomed forth.

"Then something happened on board the steamer. The figures

came to the side. I waved my coat and danced. Then they saw us.

"I was pretty well done up when they took us aboard, and I slept for twenty-four hours straight. When I awoke there sat Gulliver by my bunk, and when I turned to look at him he lifted a great paw and put it on my arm."

Enderby ceased, and there was silence in the room save for the light snoring of Nubbins.

"You took him home with you, I suppose?" I asked.

Enderby nodded.

"And you have him still?" I certainly wanted to have a look at that dog.

But he did not answer. I saw an expression of great sadness come into his eyes as he gazed out of the window, and I knew that Jacob Enderby had finished his story.

Sunning

JAMES S. TIPPETT

Old dog lay in the summer sun
Much too lazy to rise and run.
He flapped an ear
At a buzzing fly.
He winked a half opened
Sleepy eye,
He scratched himself
On an itching spot,
As he dozed on the porch

Where the sun was hot.
He whimpered a bit
From force of habit
While he lazily dreamed
Of chasing a rabbit.
But Old Dog happily lay in the sun
Much too lazy to rise and run.

Notice Given

BERTON BRALEY

I'm in disgrace
   and degradation
And yet I *told* Them
   The situation
I whined a lot
   And walked the floor
And went and sat
   By the outer door.

But They weren't paying
   The least attention,
They didn't hear
   What I tried to mention,
They wouldn't listen
   To my sad yelp

—So then what happened
I couldn't help!

I gave Them hints
And if They scorn them
They cannot say
That I didn't warn Them!

The Dog of Pompeii
LOUIS UNTERMEYER

Tito and his dog Bimbo lived (if you could call it living) under the wall where it joined the inner gate. They really didn't live there; they just slept there. They lived anywhere. Pompeii was one of the gayest of the old Latin towns, but although Tito was never an unhappy boy, he was not exactly a merry one. The streets were always lively with shining chariots and bright red trappings; the open-air theatres rocked with laughing crowds; sham-battles and athletic sports were free for the asking in the great stadium. Once a year the Caesar visited the pleasure-city and the fire-works lasted for days; the sacrifices in the Forum were better than a show. But Tito saw none of these things. He was blind—had been blind from birth. He was known to everyone in the poorer quarters. But no one could say how old he was, no one remembered his parents, no one could tell where he came from. Bimbo was another mystery. As long as people could remember seeing Tito—about twelve or thirteen years—they had seen Bimbo. Bimbo had never left his side. He was not only dog, but nurse, pillow, playmate, mother and father to Tito.

Did I say Bimbo never left his master? (Perhaps I had better say comrade, for if any one was the master, it was Bimbo.) I was wrong. Bimbo did trust Tito alone exactly three times a day. It was a fixed routine, a custom understood between boy and dog since the beginning of their friendship, and the way it worked was this: Early in the morning, shortly after dawn, while Tito was still dreaming, Bimbo would disappear. When Tito awoke, Bimbo would be sitting quietly at his side, his ears cocked, his stump of a tail tapping the ground, and a fresh-baked bread— more like a large round roll—at his feet. Tito would stretch himself; Bimbo would yawn; then they would breakfast. At noon, no matter where they happened to be, Bimbo would put his paw on Tito's knee and the two of them would return to the inner gate. Tito would curl up in the corner (almost like a dog) and go to sleep, while Bimbo, looking quite important (almost like a boy) would disappear again. In half an hour he'd be back with their lunch. Sometimes it would be a piece of fruit or a scrap of meat, often it was nothing but a dry crust. But sometimes there would be one of those flat rich cakes, sprinkled with raisins and sugar, that Tito liked so much. At supper-time the same thing happened, although there was a little less of everything, for things were hard to snatch in the evening with the streets full of people. Besides, Bimbo didn't approve of too much food before going to sleep. A heavy supper made boys too restless and dogs too stodgy—and it was the business of a dog to sleep lightly with one ear open and muscles ready for action.

But, whether there was much or little, hot or cold, fresh or dry, food was always there. Tito never asked where it came from and Bimbo never told him. There was plenty of rain-water in the hollows of soft stones; the old egg-woman at the corner some-times gave him a cupful of strong goat's milk; in the grape-season the fat wine-maker let him have drippings of the mild juice. So there was no danger of going hungry or thirsty. There was plenty of everything in Pompeii—if you knew where to find it—and if you had a dog like Bimbo.

As I said before, Tito was not the merriest boy in Pompeii. He could not romp with the other youngsters and play Hare-and-Hounds and I-spy and Follow-your-Master and Ball-against-the-

Building and lack-stones and Kings-and-Robbers with them. But that did not make him sorry for himself. If he could not see the sights that delighted the lads of Pompeii he could hear and smell things they never noticed. He could really see more with his ears and nose than they could with their eyes. When he and Bimbo went out walking he knew just where they were going and exactly what was happening.

"Ah," he'd sniff and say, as they passed a handsome villa, "Glaucus Pansa is giving a grand dinner tonight. They're going to have three kinds of bread, and roast pigling, and stuffed goose, and a great stew—I think bear-stew—and a fig-pie." And Bimbo would note that this would be a good place to visit tomorrow.

Or, "H'm," Tito would murmur, half through his lips, half through his nostrils. "The wife of Marcus Lucretius is expecting her mother. She's shaking out every piece of goods in the house; she's going to use the best clothes—the ones she's been keeping in pine-needles and camphor—and there's an extra girl in the kitchen. Come, Bimbo, let's get out of the dust!"

Or, as they passed a small but elegant dwelling opposite the public-baths, "Too bad! The tragic poet is ill again. It must be a bad fever this time, for they're trying smoke-fumes instead of medicine. Whew! I'm glad I'm not a tragic poet!"

Or, as they neared the Forum, "Mm-m! What good things they have in the Macellum today!" (It really was a sort of butcher-grocer-market-place, but Tito didn't know any better. He called it the Macellum.) "Dates from Africa, and salt oysters from sea-caves, and cuttlefish, and new honey, and sweet onions, and—ugh!—water-buffalo steaks. Come, let's see what's what in the Forum." And Bimbo, just as curious as his comrade, hurried on. Being a dog, he trusted his ears and nose (like Tito) more than his eyes. And so the two of them entered the center of Pompeii.

The Forum was the part of the town to which everybody came at least once during each day. It was the Central Square and everything happened here. There were no private houses; all was public—the chief temples, the gold and red bazaars, the silk-shops, the town-hall, the booths belonging to the weavers and jewel-merchants, the wealthy woolen market, the shrine of the household gods. Everything glittered here. The buildings looked as if they were new—which, in a sense, they were. The earthquake of twelve years ago had brought down all the old structures and, since the citizens of Pompeii were ambitious to rival Naples and even Rome, they had seized the opportunity to rebuild the whole town. And they had done it all within a dozen years. There was scarcely a building that was older than Tito.

Tito had heard a great deal about the earthquake though, being about a year old at the time, he could scarcely remember it. This particular quake had been a light one—as earthquakes go. The weaker houses had been shaken down, parts of the out-worn wall had been wrecked; but there was little loss of life, and the brilliant new Pompeii had taken the place of the old. No one knew what caused these earthquakes. Records showed they had happened in the neighborhood since the beginning of time. Sailors said that it was to teach the lazy city-folk a lesson and make them appreciate those who risked the dangers of the sea to bring them luxuries and protect their town from invaders. The priests said that the gods took this way of showing their anger to those who refused to worship properly and who failed to bring enough sacrifices to the altars and (though they didn't say it in so many words) presents to the priests. The tradesmen said that the foreign merchants had corrupted the ground and it was no longer safe to traffic in imported goods that came from strange places and carried a curse with them. Every one had a different explanation—and every one's explanation was louder and sillier than his neighbor's.

They were talking about it this afternoon as Tito and Bimbo came out of the side-street into the public square. The Forum was the favorite promenade for rich and poor. What with the priests arguing with the politicians, servants doing the day's shopping, tradesmen crying their wares, women displaying the latest fashions from Greece and Egypt, children playing hide-and-seek among the marble columns, knots of soldiers, sailors, peasants from the provinces—to say nothing of those who merely came to lounge and look on—the square was crowded to its last inch. His ears even more than his nose guided Tito to the place where the talk was loudest. It was in front of the Shrine of the Household Gods that, naturally enough, the householders were arguing.

"I tell you," rumbled a voice which Tito recognized as bathmaster Rufus's, "there won't be another earthquake in my lifetime or yours. There may be a tremble or two, but earthquakes, like lightnings, never strike twice in the same place."

"Do they not?" asked a thin voice Tito had never heard. It had a high, sharp ring to it and Tito knew it was the accent of a stranger. "How about the two towns of Sicily that have been ruined three times within fifteen years by the eruptions of Mount Etna? And were they not warned? And does that column of smoke above Vesuvius mean nothing?"

"That?" Tito could hear the grunt with which one question answered another. "That's always there. We use it for our weather-guide. When the smoke stands up straight we know we'll have fair weather; when it flattens out it's sure to be foggy; when it drifts to the east—"

"Yes, yes," cut in the edged voice. "I've heard about your mountain barometer. But the column of smoke seems hundreds of feet higher than usual and it's thickening and spreading like a shadowy tree. They say in Naples—"

"Oh, Naples!" Tito knew this voice by the little squeak that went with it. It was Attilio, the cameo-cutter. "They talk while we suffer. Little help we got from them last time. Naples commits the crimes and Pompeii pays the price. It's become a proverb with us. Let them mind their own business."

"Yes," grumbled Rufus, "and others, too."

"Very well, my confident friends," responded the thin voice which now sounded curiously flat. "We also have a proverb— and it is this: Those who will not listen to men must be taught by the gods. I say no more. But I leave a last warning. Remember the holy ones. Look to your temples. And when the smoke-tree above Vesuvius grows to the shape of an umbrella-pine, look to your lives."

Tito could hear the air whistle as the speaker drew his toga about him and the quick shuffle of feet told him the stranger had gone.

"Now what," said the cameo-cutter, "did he mean by that?"

"I wonder," grunted Rufus, "I wonder."

Tito wondered, too. And Bimbo, his head at a thoughtful angle, looked as if he had been doing a heavy piece of pondering. By nightfall the argument had been forgotten. If the smoke had increased no one saw it in the dark. Besides, it was Caesar's birthday and the town was in holiday mood. Tito and Bimbo were among the merry-makers, dodging the charioteers who shouted at them. A dozen times they almost upset baskets of sweets and jars of Vesuvian wine, said to be as fiery as the streams inside the volcano, and a dozen times they were cursed and cuffed. But Tito never missed his footing. He was thankful for his keen ears and quick instinct—most thankful of all for Bimbo.

They visited the uncovered theatre and, though Tito could not see the faces of the actors, he could follow the play better than most of the audience, for their attention wandered—they were distracted by the scenery, the costumes, the by-play, even by themselves—while Tito's whole attention was centered in what he heard. Then to the city-walls, where the people of Pompeii watched a mock naval-battle in which the city was attacked by the sea and saved after thousands of flaming arrows had been exchanged and countless colored torches had been burned. Though the thrill of flaring ships and lighted skies was lost to Tito, the shouts and cheers excited him as much as any and he cried out with the loudest of them.

The next morning there were two of the beloved raisin and sugar cakes for his breakfast. Bimbo was unusually active and thumped his bit of a tail until Tito was afraid he would wear it out. The boy could not imagine whether Bimbo was urging him to some sort of game or was trying to tell something. After a while, he ceased to notice Bimbo. He felt drowsy. Last night's late hours had tired him. Besides, there was a heavy mist in the air—no, a thick fog rather than a mist—a fog that got into his throat and scraped it and made him cough. He walked as far as the marine gate to get a breath of the sea. But the blanket of haze had spread all over the bay and even the salt air seemed smoky.

He went to bed before dusk and slept. But he did not sleep well. He had too many dreams—dreams of ships lurching in the Forum, of losing his way in a screaming crowd, of armies marching across his chest, of being pulled over every rough pavement of Pompeii.

He woke early. Or, rather, he was pulled awake. Bimbo was doing the pulling. The dog had dragged Tito to his feet and was urging the boy along. Somewhere. Where, Tito did not know. His feet stumbled uncertainly; he was still half asleep. For a while he noticed nothing except the fact that it was hard to breathe. The air was hot. And heavy. So heavy that he could taste it. The air, it seemed, had turned to powder, a warm powder that stung his nostrils and burned his sightless eyes.

Then he began to hear sounds. Peculiar sounds. Like animals under the earth. Hissings and groanings and muffled cries that a dying creature might make dislodging the stones of his underground cave. There was no doubt of it now. The noises came from underneath. He not only heard them—he could feel them. The earth twitched; the twitching changed to an uneven shrugging of the soil. Then, as Bimbo half-pulled, half-coaxed him across, the ground jerked away from his feet and he was thrown against a stone-fountain.

The water—hot water—splashing in his face revived him. He got to his feet, Bimbo steadying him, helping him on again. The noises grew louder; they came closer. The cries were even more animal-like than before, but now they came from human throats. A few people, quicker of foot and more hurried by fear, began to rush by. A family or two—then a section—then, it seemed, an army broken out of bounds. Tito, bewildered though he was, could recognize Rufus as he bellowed past him, like a water-buffalo gone mad. Time was lost in a nightmare.

It was then the crashing began. First a sharp crackling, like a monstrous snapping of twigs; then a roar like the fall of a whole forest of trees; then an explosion that tore earth and sky. The heavens, though Tito could not see them, were shot through with continual flickerings of fire. Lightnings above were answered by thunders beneath. A house fell. Then another. By a miracle the two companions had escaped the dangerous side-streets and were in a more open space. It was the Forum. They rested here a while—how long he did not know.

Tito had no idea of the time of day. He could feel it was black—
an unnatural blackness. Something inside—perhaps the lack of
breakfast and lunch—told him it was past noon. But it didn't matter.
Nothing seemed to matter. He was getting drowsy, too drowsy
to walk. But walk he must. He knew it. And Bimbo knew it; the
sharp tugs told him so. Nor was it a moment too soon. The sacred
ground of the Forum was safe no longer. It was beginning to
rock, then to pitch, then to split. As they stumbled out of the
square, the earth wriggled like a caught snake and all the columns
of the temple of Jupiter came down. It was the end of the world—
or so it seemed. To walk was not enough now. They must run.
Tito was too frightened to know what to do or where to go. He
had lost all sense of direction. He started to go back to the inner
gate; but Bimbo, straining his back to the last inch, almost pulled
his clothes from him. What did the creature want? Had the dog
gone mad?

Then, suddenly, he understood. Bimbo was telling him the way
out—urging him there. The sea-gate of course. The sea-gate—
and then the sea. Far from falling buildings, heaving ground. He
turned, Bimbo guiding him across open pits and dangerous pools
of bubbling mud, away from buildings that had caught fire and
were dropping their burning beams. Tito could no longer tell
whether the noises were made by the shrieking sky or the agonized
people. He and Bimbo ran on—the only silent beings in a howling
world.

New dangers threatened. All Pompeii seemed to be thronging
toward the marine-gate and, squeezing among the crowds, there
was the chance of being trampled to death. But the chance had
to be taken. It was growing harder and harder to breathe. What
air there was choked him. It was all dust now—dust and pebbles,
pebbles as large as beans. They fell on his head, his hands—pumice-
stones from the black heart of Vesuvius. The mountain was turning
itself inside out. Tito remembered a phrase that the stranger had
said in the Forum two days ago: "Those who will not listen to
men must be taught by the gods." The people of Pompeii had
refused to heed the warnings; they were being taught now—if it
was not too late.

Suddenly it seemed too late for Tito. The red hot ashes blistered his skin, the stinging vapors tore his throat. He could not go on. He staggered toward a small tree at the side of the road and fell. In a moment Bimbo was beside him. He coaxed. But there was no answer. He licked Tito's hands, his feet, his face. The boy did not stir. Then Bimbo did the last thing he could—the last thing he wanted to do. He bit his comrade, bit him deep in the arm. With a cry of pain, Tito jumped to his feet, Bimbo after him. Tito was in despair, but Bimbo was determined. He drove the boy on, snapping at his heels, worrying his way through the crowd; barking, baring his teeth, heedless of kicks or falling stones. Sick with hunger, half-dead with fear and sulphur-fumes, Tito pounded on, pursued by Bimbo. How long he never knew. At last he staggered through the marine-gate and felt soft sand under him. Then Tito fainted . . .

Some one was dashing sea-water over him. Some one was carrying him toward a boat.

"Bimbo," he called. And then louder, "Bimbo!" But Bimbo had disappeared.

Voices jarred against each other. "Hurry—hurry!" "To the boats!" "Can't you see the child's frightened and starving!" "He keeps calling for some one!" "Poor boy, he's out of his mind." "Here, child—take this!"

They tucked him in among them. The oar-locks creaked; the oars splashed; the boat rode over toppling waves. Tito was safe. But he wept continually.

"Bimbo!" he wailed. "Bimbo! Bimbo!"

He could not be comforted.

Eighteen hundred years passed. Scientists were restoring the ancient city; excavators were working their way through the stones and trash that had buried the entire town. Much had already been brought to light—statues, bronze instruments, bright mosaics, household articles; even delicate paintings had been preserved by the fall of ashes that had taken over two thousand lives. Columns were dug up and the Forum was beginning to emerge.

It was at a place where the ruins lay deepest that the Director paused.

"Come here," he called to his assistant. "I think we've discovered the remains of a building in good shape. Here are four huge mill-stones that were most likely turned by slaves or mules—and here is a whole wall standing with shelves inside it. Why! It must have been a bakery. And here's a curious thing. What do you think I found under this heap where the ashes were thickest? The skeleton of a dog!"

"Amazing!" gasped his assistant. "You'd think a dog would have had sense enough to run away at the time. And what is that flat thing he's holding between his teeth? It can't be a stone."

"No. It must have come from this bakery. You know it looks to me like some sort of cake hardened with the years. And, bless me, if those little black pebbles aren't raisins. A raisin-cake almost two thousand years old! I wonder what made him want it at such a moment?"

"I wonder," murmured the assistant.

A Dog's Life

MILLY WALTON

I'm sick of all this silly rot,
Pooches today are a pampered lot;
Doggie diets, doggie dinners
(Guaranteeing ribbon winners);
People to clip and comb my coat,
A sissy collar for my throat
A pillow for my doggie bed
(It's shame that makes me hang my head).
Wearing a sweater was pretty bad,

But doggie boots will drive me mad;
I eat my meals from a special dish
When all in the world I really wish
Is a dirty old bone and a yard so big
It would take a pup's lifetime just to dig.
I'd get into fights and play with kids
And do the things my ancestors did;
I would have a doghouse all my own
And sleep outside at night alone!
But who am I to long for a lark
When I'm not allowed to have even a bark?

"Old Bob—Friend"

MARTY HALE

To some folks he was just a dog,
An ordinary hound—
Who ambled up and down the streets
And raked about the town;
The smoke and black of city streets
Had somewhat dulled his fur;
And not a one who knew Old Bob
Would speak of him as 'Cur.'

He was a gentleman at heart,
He stopped beside your door
And took the bite you offered him,
And wagged his tail for more;

A look of deepest gratitude
Shone in his patient eyes—
His was a heart of purest gold,
And love had made him wise.

Old Bob was laid away today
Beneath a mound of flowers,
And sleep has ended sufferings
Of many weary hours.
A traffic victim, Old Bob lay,
His body racked with pain,
And all that tender hands could do
To save him, was in vain.

Amid a city's roar and din,
And all the rush of day,
A silence veiled the old back-yard
As Bob was laid away.
And fifty men and women stood
About his humble bier,
And watched the quiet old gaunt form,
And wiped away a tear.

And so with quiet reverence,
Old Bob was laid to rest,
To live forever in the hearts
Of those who knew him best.
He loved his neighbors as himself,
Nor stooped to once offend—
No other so deserves to have
Folks speak of him as—FRIEND.

For the Love of a Man
JACK LONDON

When John Thornton froze his feet in the previous December, his partners had made him comfortable and left him to get well, going on themselves up the river to get out a raft of saw-logs for Dawson. He was still limping slightly at the time he rescued Buck, but with the continued warm weather even the slight limp left him. And here, lying by the river bank through the long spring days, watching the running water, listening lazily to the songs of birds and the hum of nature, Buck slowly won back his strength.

A rest comes very good after one has travelled three thousand miles, and it must be confessed that Buck waxed lazy as his wounds healed, his muscles swelled out, and the flesh came back to cover his bones. For that matter, they were all loafing—Buck, John Thornton, and Skeet and Nig—waiting for the raft to come that was to carry them down to Dawson. Skeet was a little Irish setter who early made friends with Buck, who, in a dying condition, was unable to resent her first advances. She had the doctor trait which some dogs possess, and as a mother cat washes her kittens, so she washed and cleansed Buck's wounds. Regularly, each morning after he had finished his breakfast, she performed her self-appointed task, till he came to look for her ministrations as much as he did for Thornton's. Nig, equally friendly, though less demonstrative, was a huge black dog, half bloodhound and half deerhound, with eyes that laughed and a boundless good nature.

To Buck's surprise these dogs manifested no jealousy toward him. They seemed to share the kindliness and largeness of John Thornton. As Buck grew stronger they enticed him into all sorts of ridiculous games, in which Thornton himself could not forbear to join, and in this fashion Buck romped through his convalescence and into a new existence. Love, genuine passionate love, was his for the first time. This he had never experienced at Judge Miller's down in the sun-kissed Santa Clara Valley. With the Judge's sons, hunting and tramping, it had been a working partnership; with the Judge's grandsons, a sort of pompous guardianship; and with the Judge himself, a stately and dignified friendship. But love that was feverish and burning, that was adoration, that was madness, it had taken John Thornton to arouse.

This man had saved his life, which was something; but, further, he was the ideal master. Other men saw to the welfare of their dogs from a sense of duty and business expediency; he saw to the welfare of his as if they were his own children, because he could not help it. And he saw further. He never forgot a kindly greeting or a cheering word, and to sit down for a long talk with them ("gas" he called it) was as much his delight as theirs. He had a way of taking Buck's head roughly between his hands, and resting his own head upon Buck's, of shaking him back and forth, the while calling him ill names that to Buck were love names. Buck knew no greater joy than that rough embrace and the sound of murmured oaths, and at each jerk back and forth it seemed that his heart would be shaken out of his body so great was his ecstasy. And when, released, he sprang to his feet, his mouth laughing, his eyes eloquent, his throat vibrant with unuttered sound, and in that fashion remained without movement, John Thornton would reverently exclaim, "God! you can all but speak!"

Buck had a trick of love expression that was akin to hurt. He would often seize Thornton's hand in his mouth and close so fiercely that the flesh bore the impress of his teeth for some time afterward. And as Buck understood the oaths to be love words, so the man understood this feigned bite for a caress.

For the most part, however, Buck's love was expressed in adoration. While he went wild with happiness when Thornton touched him or spoke to him, he did not seek these tokens. Unlike Skeet, who was wont to shove her nose under Thornton's hand and nudge and nudge till petted, or Nig, who would stalk up and rest his great head on Thornton's knee, Buck was content to adore at a distance. He would lie by the hour, eager, alert, at Thornton's feet, looking up into his face, dwelling upon it, studying it, following with keenest interest each fleeting expression, every movement or change of feature. Or, as chance might have it, he would lie farther away, to the side or rear, watching the outlines of the man and the occasional movements of his body. And often, such was the communion in which they lived, the strength of Buck's gaze would draw John Thornton's head around, and he would return the gaze, without speech, his heart shining out of his eyes as Buck's heart shone out.

For a long time after his rescue, Buck did not like Thornton to get out of his sight. From the moment he left the tent to when he entered it again, Buck would follow at his heels. His transient masters since he had come into the Northland had bred in him a fear that no master could be permanent. He was afraid that Thornton would pass out of his life as Perrault and François and the Scotch half-breed had passed out. Even in the night, in his dreams, he was haunted by this fear. At such times he would shake off sleep and creep through the chill to the flap of the tent, where he would stand and listen to the sound of his master's breathing.

But in spite of this great love he bore John Thornton, which seemed to bespeak the soft civilizing influence, the strain of the primitive, which the Northland had aroused in him, remained alive and active. Faithfulness and devotion, things born of fire and roof, were his; yet he retained his wildness and wiliness. He was a thing of the wild, come in from the wild to sit by John Thornton's fire, rather than a dog of the soft Southland stamped with the marks of generations of civilization. Because of his very great love, he could not steal from this man, but from any other man, in any other camp, he did not hesitate an instant; while the cunning with which he stole enabled him to escape detection.

His face and body were scored by the teeth of many dogs, and he fought as fiercely as ever and more shrewdly. Skeet and Nig were too good-natured for quarrelling—besides, they belonged to John Thornton; but the strange dog, no matter what the breed or valor, swiftly acknowledged Buck's supremacy or found himself struggling for life with a terrible antagonist. And Buck was merciless. He had learned well the law of club and fang, and he never forewent an advantage or drew back from a foe he had started on the way to Death. He had lessoned from Spitz, and from the chief fighting dogs of the police and mail, and knew there was no middle course. He must master or be mastered; while to show mercy was a weakness. Mercy did not exist in the primordial life. It was misunderstood for fear, and such misunderstandings made for death. Kill or be killed, eat or be eaten, was the law; and this mandate, down out of the depths of Time, he obeyed.

He was older than the days he had seen and the breaths he had drawn. He linked the past with the present, and the eternity behind him throbbed through him in a mighty rhythm to which he swayed as the tides and seasons swayed. He sat by John Thornton's fire, a broad-breasted dog, white-fanged and long-furred; but behind him were the shades of all manner of dogs, half-wolves and wild wolves, urgent and prompting, tasting the savor of the meat he ate, thirsting for the water he drank, scenting the wind with him, listening with him and telling him the sounds made by the wild life in the forest, dictating his moods, directing his actions, lying down to sleep with him when he lay down, and dreaming with him and beyond him and becoming themselves the stuff of his dreams.

So peremptorily did these shades beckon him that each day mankind and the claims of mankind slipped farther from him. Deep in the forest a call was sounding, and as often as he heard this call, mysteriously thrilling and luring, he felt compelled to turn his back upon the fire and the beaten earth around it, and to plunge into the forest, and on and on, he knew not where or why; nor did he wonder where or why, the call sounding imperiously, deep in the forest. But as often as he gained the soft unbroken earth and the green shade, the love for John Thornton drew him back to the fire again.

Thornton alone held him. The rest of mankind was as nothing. Chance travellers might praise or pet him; but he was cold under it all, and from a too demonstrative man he would get up and walk away. When Thornton's partners, Hans and Pete, arrived on the long-expected raft, Buck refused to notice them till he learned they were close to Thornton; after that he tolerated them in a passive sort of way, accepting favors from them as though he favored them by accepting. They were of the same large type as Thornton, living close to the earth, thinking simply and seeing clearly; and ere they swung the raft into the big eddy by the saw-mill at Dawson, they understood Buck and his ways, and did not insist upon an intimacy such as obtained with Skeet and Nig.

For Thornton, however, his love seemed to grow and grow. He, alone among men, could put a pack upon Buck's back in the summer travelling. Nothing was too great for Buck to do, when Thornton commanded. One day (they had grub-staked themselves from the proceeds of the raft and left Dawson for the head-waters of the Tanana) the men and dogs were sitting on the crest of a cliff which fell away, straight down, to naked bed-rock three hundred feet below. John Thornton was sitting near the edge, Buck at his shoulder. A thoughtless whim seized Thornton, and he drew the attention of Hans and Pete to the experiment he had in mind. "Jump, Buck!" he commanded, sweeping his arm out and over the chasm. The next instant he was grappling with Buck on the extreme edge, while Hans and Pete were dragging them back into safety.

"It's uncanny," Pete said, after it was over and they had caught their speech.

Thornton shook his head. "No, it is splendid, and it is terrible, too. Do you know, it sometimes makes me afraid."

"I'm not hankering to be the man that lays hands on you while he's around," Pete announced conclusively, nodding his head toward Buck.

"Py jingo!" was Hans' contribution. "Not mineself either."

It was at Circle City, ere the year was out, that Pete's apprehensions were realized. "Black" Burton, a man evil-tempered and malicious, had been picking a quarrel with a tenderfoot at the bar, when Thornton stepped good-naturedly between. Buck, as was his custom, was lying in a corner, head on paws, watching his master's every action. Burton struck out, without warning, straight from the shoulder. Thornton was sent spinning, and saved himself from falling only by clutching the rail of the bar.

Those who were looking on heard what was neither bark nor yelp, but a something which is best described as a roar, and they saw Buck's body rise up in the air as he left the floor for Burton's throat. The man saved his life by instinctively throwing out his arm, but was hurled backward to the floor with Buck on top of him. Buck loosed his teeth from the flesh of the arm and drove in again for the throat. This time the man succeeded only in partly blocking, and his throat was torn open. Then the crowd was upon Buck, and he was driven off; but while a surgeon checked the bleeding, he prowled up and down, growling furiously, attempting to rush in, and being forced back by an array of hostile clubs. A "miners' meeting," called on the spot, decided that the dog had sufficient provocation, and Buck was discharged. But his reputation was made, and from that day his name spread through every camp in Alaska.

Later on, in the fall of the year, he saved John Thornton's life in quite another fashion. The three partners were lining a long and narrow poling-boat down a bad stretch of rapids on the Forty-Mile Creek. Hans and Pete moved along the bank, snubbing with a thin Manila rope from tree to tree, while Thornton remained in the boat, helping its descent by means of a pole, and shouting directions to the shore. Buck, on the bank, worried and anxious, kept abreast of the boat, his eyes never off his master.

At a particularly bad spot, where a ledge of barely submerged rocks jutted out into the river, Hans cast off the rope, and, while Thornton poled the boat out into the stream, ran down the bank with the end in his hand to snub the boat when it had cleared the ledge. This it did, and was flying down-stream in a current as swift as a mill-race, when Hans checked it with the rope and checked too suddenly. The boat flirted over and snubbed in to the bank bottom up, while Thornton, flung sheer out of it, was carried down-stream toward the worst part of the rapids, a stretch of wild water in which no swimmer could live.

Buck had sprung in on the instant, and at the end of three

hundred yards, amid a mad swirl of water, he overhauled Thornton. When he felt him grasp his tail, Buck headed for the bank, swimming with all his splendid strength. But the progress shoreward was slow; the progress down-stream amazingly rapid. From below came the fatal roaring where the wild current went wilder and was rent in shreds and spray by the rocks which thrust through like the teeth of an enormous comb. The suck of the water as it took the beginning of the last steep pitch was frightful, and Thornton knew that the shore was impossible. He scraped furiously over a rock, bruised across a second, and struck a third with crushing force. He clutched its slippery top with both hands, releasing Buck, and above the roar of the churning water shouted: "Go, Buck! Go!"

Buck could not hold his own, and swept on down-stream, struggling desperately, but unable to win back. When he heard Thornton's command repeated, he partly reared out of the water, throwing his head high, as though for a last look, then turned obediently toward the bank. He swam powerfully and was dragged ashore by Pete and Hans at the very point where swimming ceased to be possible and destruction began.

They knew that the time a man could cling to a slippery rock in the face of that driving current was a matter of minutes, and they ran as fast as they could up the bank to a point far above where Thornton was hanging on. They attached the line with which they had been snubbing the boat to Buck's neck and shoulders, being careful that it should neither strangle him nor impede his swimming, and launched him into the stream. He struck out boldly, but not straight enough into the stream. He discovered the mistake too late, when Thornton was abreast of him and a bare half-dozen strokes away while he was being carried helplessly past.

Hans promptly snubbed with the rope, as though Buck were a boat. The rope thus tightening on him in the sweep of the current, he was jerked under the surface, and under the surface he remained till his body struck against the bank and he was hauled out. He was half drowned, and Hans and Pete threw themselves upon him, pounding the breath into him and the water out of him. He staggered to his feet and fell down. The faint sound of Thornton's voice came to them, and though they could not make out the words of it, they knew that he was in his extremity. His master's voice acted on Buck like an electric shock. He sprang to his feet and ran up the bank ahead of the men to the point of his previous departure.

Again the rope was attached and he was launched, and again he struck out, but this time straight into the stream. He had miscalculated once, but he would not be guilty of it a second time. Hans paid out the rope, permitting no slack while Pete kept it clear of coils. Buck held on till he was on a line straight above Thornton; then he turned, and with the speed of an express train headed down upon him. Thornton saw him coming, and, as Buck struck him like a battering ram, with the whole force of the current behind him, he reached up and closed with both arms around the shaggy neck. Hans snubbed the rope around the tree, and Buck and Thornton were jerked under the water. Strangling, suffocating, sometimes one uppermost and sometimes the other, dragging over the jagged bottom, smashing against rocks and snags, they veered in to the bank.

Thornton came to, belly downward and being violently propelled back and forth across a drift log by Hans and Pete. His first glance was for Buck, over whose limp and apparently lifeless body Nig was setting up a howl, while Skeet was licking the wet face and closed eyes. Thornton was himself bruised and battered, and he went carefully over Buck's body, when he had been brought around, finding three broken ribs.

"That settles it," he announced. "We camp right here." And camp they did, till Buck's ribs knitted and he was able to travel.

That winter, at Dawson, Buck performed another exploit, not so heroic, perhaps, but one that put his name many notches higher on the totem-pole of Alaskan fame. This exploit was particularly gratifying to the three men; for they stood in need of the outfit which it furnished, and were enabled to make a long-desired trip into the virgin East, where miners had not yet appeared. It was brought about by a conversation in the Eldorado Saloon, in which men waxed boastful of their favorite dogs. Buck, because of his record, was the target for these men, and Thornton was driven stoutly to defend him. At the end of half an hour one man stated that his dog could start a sled with five hundred pounds and walk off with it; a second bragged six hundred for his dog; and a third seven hundred.

"Pooh! pooh!" said John Thornton. "Buck can start a thousand pounds."

"And break it out? and walk off with it for a hundred yards?" demanded Matthewson, a Bonanza King, he of the seven hundred vaunt.

"And break it out, and walk off with it for a hundred yards," John Thornton said coolly.

"Well," Matthewson said, slowly and deliberately, so that all could hear, "I've got a thousand dollars that says he can't. And there it is." So saying, he slammed a sack of gold dust of the size of a bologna sausage down upon the bar.

Nobody spoke. Thornton's bluff, if bluff it was, had been called. He could feel a flush of warm blood creeping up his face. His tongue had tricked him. He did not know whether Buck could start a thousand pounds. Half a ton! The enormousness of it appalled him. He had great faith in Buck's strength and had often thought him capable of starting such a load; but never, as now, had he faced the possibility of it, the eyes of a dozen men fixed upon him, silent and waiting. Further, he had no thousand dollars; nor had Hans or Pete.

"I've got a sled standing outside now, with twenty fifty-pound sacks of flour on it," Matthewson went on with brutal directness, "so don't let that hinder you."

Thornton did not reply. He did not know what to say. He glanced from face to face in the absent way of a man who has lost the power of thought and is seeking somewhere to find the thing that will start it going again. The face of Jim O'Brien, a Mastodon King and old-time comrade, caught his eyes. It was as a cue to him, seeming to rouse him to do what he would never have dreamed of doing.

"Can you lend me a thousand?" he asked, almost in a whisper.

"Sure," answered O'Brien, thumping down a plethoric sack by the side of Matthewson's. "Though it's little faith I'm having, John, that the beast can do the trick."

The Eldorado emptied its occupants into the street to see the test. The tables were deserted, and the dealers and game-keepers came forth to see the outcome of the wager and to lay odds. Several hundred men, furred and mittened, banked around the sled within easy distance. Matthewson's sled, loaded with a thousand pounds of flour, had been standing for a couple of hours, and in the intense cold (it was sixty below zero) the runners had frozen fast to the hard-packed snow. Men offered odds of two to one that Buck could not budge the sled. A quibble arose concerning the phrase "break out." O'Brien contended it was Thornton's privilege to knock the runners loose, leaving Buck to "break it out" from a dead standstill. Matthewson insisted that the phrase included breaking the runners from the frozen grip of the snow. A majority of the men who had witnessed the making of the bet decided in his favor, whereat the odds went up to three to one against Buck.

There were no takers. Not a man believed him capable of the feat. Thornton had been hurried into the wager, heavy with doubt; and now that he looked at the sled itself, the concrete fact, with the regular team of ten dogs curled up in the snow before it, the more impossible the task appeared. Matthewson waxed jubilant.

"Three to one!" he proclaimed. "I'll lay you another thousand at that figure, Thornton. What d'ye say?"

Thornton's doubt was strong in his face, but his fighting spirit was aroused—the fighting spirit that soars above odds, fails to recognize the impossible, and is deaf to all save the clamor for battle. He called Hans and Pete to him. Their sacks were slim, and with his own the three partners could rake together only two hundred dollars. In the ebb of their fortunes, this sum was their total capital; yet they laid it unhesitatingly against Matthewson's six hundred.

The team of ten dogs was unhitched, and Buck, with his own harness, was put into the sled. He had caught the contagion of the excitement, and he felt that in some way he must do a great thing for John Thornton. Murmurs of admiration at his splendid appearance went up. He was in perfect condition, without an ounce of superfluous flesh, and the one hundred and fifty pounds that he weighed were so many pounds of grit and virility. His furry coat shone with the sheen of silk. Down the neck and across the shoulders, his mane, in repose as it was, half bristled and seemed to lift with every movement, as though excess of vigor made each particular hair alive and active. The great breast and heavy fore legs were no more than in proportion with the rest of the body, where the muscles showed in tight rolls underneath the skin. Men felt these muscles and proclaimed them hard as iron, and the odds went down to two to one.

"Gad, sir! Gad, sir!" stuttered a member of the latest dynasty, a king of the Skookum Benches. "I offer you eight hundred for him, sir, before the test, sir; eight hundred just as he stands."

Thornton shook his head and stepped to Buck's side.

"You must stand off from him," Matthewson protested. "Free play and plenty of room."

The crowd fell silent; only could be heard the voices of the gamblers vainly offering two to one. Everybody acknowledged Buck a magnificent animal, but twenty fifty-pound sacks of flour bulked too large in their eyes for them to loosen their pouch-strings.

Thornton knelt down by Buck's side. He took his head in his two hands and rested cheek on cheek. He did not playfully shake him, as was his wont, or murmur soft love curses; but he whispered in his ear. "As you love me, Buck. As you love me," was what he whispered. Buck whined with suppressed eagerness.

The crowd was watching curiously. The affair was growing mysterious. It seemed like a conjuration. As Thornton got to his feet, Buck seized his mittened hand between his jaws, pressing in with his teeth and releasing slowly, half-reluctantly. It was the answer, in terms not of speech, but of love. Thornton stepped well back.

"Now, Buck," he said.

Buck tightened the traces, then slacked them for a matter of several inches. It was the way he had learned.

"Gee!" Thornton's voice rang out, sharp in the tense silence.

Buck swung to the right, ending the movement in a plunge that took up the slack and with a sudden jerk arrested his one hundred and fifty pounds. The load quivered, and from under the runners arose a crisp crackling.

"Haw!" Thornton commanded.

Buck duplicated the maneuver, this time to the left. The crackling turned into a snapping, the sled pivoting and the runners slipping and grating several inches to the side. The sled was broken out. Men were holding their breaths, intensely unconscious of the fact.

"Now, MUSH!"

Thornton's command cracked out like a pistol-shot. Buck threw himself forward, tightening the traces with a jarring lunge. His whole body was gathered compactly together in the tremendous effort, the muscles writhing and knotting like live things under the silky fur. His great chest was low to the ground, his head forward and down, while his feet were flying like mad, the claws scarring the hard-packed snow in parallel grooves. The sled swayed and trembled, half-started forward. One of his feet slipped, and one man groaned aloud. Then the sled lurched ahead in what appeared a rapid succession of jerks, though it never really came to a dead stop again . . . half an inch . . . an inch . . . two inches. . . . The jerks perceptibly diminished; as the sled gained momentum, he caught them up, till it was moving steadily along.

Men gasped and began to breathe again, unaware that for a moment they had ceased to breathe. Thornton was running behind, encouraging Buck with short, cheery words. The distance had been measured off, and as he neared the pile of firewood which marked the end of the hundred yards, a cheer began to grow and grow, which burst into a roar as he passed the firewood and halted at command. Every man was tearing himself loose, even Matthewson. Hats and mittens were flying in the air. Men were shaking hands, it did not matter with whom, and bubbling over in a general incoherent babel.

But Thornton fell on his knees beside Buck. Head was against head, and he was shaking him back and forth. Those who hurried up heard him cursing Buck, and he cursed him long and fervently, and softly and lovingly.

"Gad, sir! Gad, sir!" spluttered the Skookum Bench king. "I'll give you a thousand for him, sir, a thousand, sir—twelve hundred, sir."

Thornton rose to his feet. His eyes were wet. The tears were streaming frankly down his cheeks. "Sir," he said to the Skookum Bench king, "no, sir. You can go to hell, sir. It's the best I can do for you, sir."

Buck seized Thornton's hand in his teeth. Thornton shook him back and forth. As though animated by a common impulse, the onlookers drew back to a respectful distance; nor were they again indiscreet enough to interrupt.

Sympathetic

BURGES JOHNSON

Whenever I start out to walk, our dog he seems to know,
　And runs along ahead of me to show he's coming too;
And when there's a reason why he really mustn't go
　The hollering "Go Home" to him is awful hard to do.

He wags his tail and jumps around, and seems as if he said,
　"I guess you didn't mean it, you were only jokin' then!"
But when he sees I'm serious he kinder droops his head,
　Or looks up at me sorrowful, an' looks away again.

And then at last he minds me if I keep an angry tone,
　It's awful hard to do it, but I try with all my might;
And sometimes when I look around I see him all alone
　A watchin' me and watchin' me until I'm out of sight.

You see I know just how it is, 'cause some days when I find
　My brother's got to hurry off with bigger boys to play,

And when he says I mustn't go and tag along behind,
He leaves me sittin' somewhere and a-feelin' just that way!

pete at the seashore
don marquis

i ran along the yellow sand
and made the sea gulls fly
i chased them down the waters edge
i chased them up the sky

i ran so hard i ran so fast
i left the spray behind
i chased the flying flecks of foam
and i outran the wind

an airplane sailing overhead
climbed when it heard me bark
i yelped and leapt right at the sun
until the sky grew dark

some little children on the beach
threw sticks and ran with me
o master let us go again
and play beside the sea

Verdun Belle

ALEXANDER WOOLLCOTT

I first heard the saga of Verdun Belle's adventure as it was being told one June afternoon under a drowsy apple tree in the troubled valley of the Marne.

The story began in a chill, grimy Lorraine village, where, in hovels and haymows, a disconsolate detachment of United States marines lay waiting the order to go up into that maze of trenches of which the crumbling traces still weave a haunted web around the citadel bearing the immortal name of Verdun.

Into this village at dusk one day in the early spring of 1918 there came out of space a shabby, lonesome dog—a squat setter of indiscreet, complex and unguessable ancestry.

One watching her as she trotted intently along the aromatic village street would have sworn that she had an important engagement with the mayor and was, regretfully, a little late.

At the end of the street she came to where a young buck private lounged glumly on a doorstep. Halting in her tracks, she sat down to contemplate him. Then satisfied seemingly by what she sensed and saw, she came over and flopped down beside him in a most companionable manner, settling herself comfortably as if she had come at last to her long journey's end. His pleased hand reached over and played with one silken chocolate-colored ear.

Somehow that gesture sealed a compact between those two. There was thereafter no doubt in either's mind that they belonged to each other for better or for worse, in sickness and in health, through weal and woe, world without end.

She ate when and what he ate. She slept beside him in the day, her muzzle resting on his leg so that he could not get up

in the night and go forgetfully back to America without her noticing it.

To the uninitiated onlookers her enthusiasm may not have been
immediately explicable. In the eyes of his top sergeant and his
company clerk he may well have seemed an undistinguished war-
rior, freckle-faced and immensely indifferent to the business of
making the world safe for democracy.

Verdun Belle thought him the most charming person in all the
world. There was a loose popular notion that she had joined up
with the company as mascot and belonged to them all. She affably
let them think so, but she had her own ideas on the subject.

When they moved up into the line she went along and was so
obviously trench-broken that they guessed she had already served
a hitch with some French regiment in that once desperate region.

They even built up the not-implausible theory that she had
come to them lonely from the grave of some little soldier in faded
horizon blue.

Certainly she knew trench ways, knew in the narrowest of pas-
sages how to keep out from underfoot and was so well aware of
the dangers of the parapet that a plate of chicken bones up there
would not have interested her. She even knew what gas was,
and after a reminding whiff of it became more than reconciled to
the regulation gas mask, which they patiently wrecked for all subse-
quent human use because an unimaginative War Department had
not foreseen the peculiar anatomical specifications of Verdun Belle.

In May, when the outfit was engaged in the exhausting activities
which the High Command was pleased to describe as "resting,"
Belle thought it a convenient time to present an interested but
amply forewarned regiment with seven wriggling casuals, some
black and white and mottled as a mackerel sky, some splotched
with the same brown as her own.

These newcomers complicated the domestic economy of the
leathernecks' haymow, but they did not become an acute problem
until that memorable night late in the month when breathless
word bade these troops be up and away.

The Second Division of the A.E.F. was always being thus picked up by the scruff of the neck and flung across France. This time the enemy had snapped up Soissons and Rheims and were pushing with dreadful ease and speed toward the remembering Marne.

Foch had called upon the Americans to help stem the tide. Ahead of the marines, as they scrambled across the monotonous plain of the Champagne, there lay amid the ripening wheat fields a mean and hilly patch of timber called Belleau Wood. Verdun Belle went along.

The leatherneck had solved the problem of the puppies by drowning four and placing the other three in a basket he had begged from a village woman.

His notion that he could carry the basket would have come as a shock to whatever functionary back in Washington designed the marine pack, which, with its near assortment of food supplies, extra clothing, emergency restoratives, and gruesome implements for destruction, had been so painstakingly calculated to exhaust the capacity of the human back. But in his need the young marine somehow contrived to add an item not in the regulations—namely, one basket containing three unweaned and faintly resentful puppies.

By night and by day the troop movement was made, now in little wheezing trains, now in swarming lorries, now afoot.

Sometimes Belle's crony rode. Sometimes (under pressure of popular clamor against the room he was taking up) he would yield up his place to the basket and jog along with his hand on the tailboard, with Belle trotting behind him.

All the soldiers in Christendom seemed to be moving across France to some nameless crossroads over the hill. Obviously this was no mere shift from one quiet sector to another. They were going to war.

Everyone had assured the stubborn youngster that he would not be able to manage, and now misgivings settled on him like crows.

He guessed that Verdun Belle must be wondering too. He turned to assure her that everything would be all right. She was not there. Ahead of him, behind him, there was no sign of her. No one within call had seen her quit the line. He kept telling himself she would show up. But the day went and the night came without her.

He jettisoned the basket and pouched the pups in his forest-green shirt in the manner of kangaroos. In the morning one of the three was dead. And the problem of transporting the other two was now tangled by the circumstance that he had to feed them.

An immensely interested old woman in the village where they halted at sunup, vastly amused by this spectacle of a soldier trying to carry two nursing puppies to war, volunteered some milk for the cup of his mess kit, and with much jeering advice from all sides, and, by dint of the eye-dropper from his pack, he tried sheepishly to be a mother to the two waifs. The attempt was not shiningly successful.

He itched to pitch them over the fence. But if Verdun Belle had not been run over by some thundering camion, if she lived she would find him, and then what would he say when her eyes asked what he had done with the pups?

So, as the order was shouted to fall in, he hitched his pack to his back and stuffed his charges back into his shirt.

Now, in the morning light, the highway was choked. Down from the lines in agonized, grotesque rout came the stream of French life from the threatened countryside, jumbled fragments of fleeing French regiments. But America was coming up the road.

It was a week in which the world held its breath.

The battle was close at hand now. Field hospitals, jostling in the river of traffic, sought space to pitch their tents. The top sergeant of one such outfit was riding on the driver's seat of an ambulance. Marines in endless number were moving up fast.

It was one of those who, in a moment's halt, fell out of line, leaped to the step of the blockaded ambulance, and looked eagerly into the medico top sergeant's eyes.

"Say, buddy," whispered the youngster, "take care of these for me. I lost their mother in the jam."

The Top found his hands closing on two drowsy pups.

All that day the field-hospital personnel was harried by the task of providing nourishment for the two casuals who had been thus unexpectedly attached to them for rations. Once established in a farmhouse (from which they were promptly shelled out), the Top went over the possible provender and found that the pups were not yet equal to a diet of bread, corn syrup and corned willy. A stray cow, loosed from her moorings in the great flight, was browsing tentatively in the next field, and two orderlies who had carelessly reminisced of life on their farms back home were detailed to induce her cooperation.

But the bombardment had brought out a certain moody goatishness in this cow, and she would not let them come near her. After a hot and maddening chase that lasted two hours, the two milkmen reported a complete failure to their disgusted chief.

The problem was still unsolved at sundown, and the pups lay faint in their bed of absorbent cotton out in the garden, when, bringing up the rear of a detachment of marines that straggled past, there trotted a brown-and-white setter.

"It would be swell if she had milk in her," the top sergeant said reflectively, wondering how he could salvage the mascot of an outfit on the march.

But his larcenous thoughts were waste. At the gate she halted dead in her tracks, flung her head high to sniff the air, wheeled sharp to the left and became just a streak of brown and white against the ground. The entire staff came out and formed a jostling circle to watch the family reunion.

After that it was tacitly assumed that these casuals belonged. When the hospital was ordered to shift further back beyond the reach of the whining shells, Verdun Belle and the pups were intrusted to an ambulance driver and went along in style. They all moved—bag, baggage and livestock—into the deserted little Chateau of the Guardian Angel, of which the front windows were curtained against the eyes and dust of the road, but of which the rear windows looked out across drooping fruit trees upon a sleepy, murmurous, multi-colored valley, fair as the Garden of the Lord.

The operating tables, with acetylene torches to light them, were set up in what had been a tool shed. Cots were strewn in the orchard alongside. Thereafter for a month there was never rest in that hospital.

The surgeons and orderlies spelled each other at times, snatching morsels of sleep and returning a few hours later to relieve the others. But Verdun Belle took no time off. Between cat naps in the corner, due attentions to her restive brood and an occasional snack for herself, she managed somehow to be on hand for every ambulance, cursorily examining each casualty as he was lifted to the ground.

Then, in the four o'clock dark of one morning, the orderly bending over a stretcher that had just been rested on the ground was hit by something that half bowled him over.

The projectile was Verdun Belle. Every quivering inch of her proclaimed to all concerned that here was a case she was personally in charge of. From nose to tail tip she was taut with excitement, and a kind of eager whimpering bubbled up out of her as if she ached to sit back on her haunches and roar to the star-spangled sky but was really too busy at the moment to indulge herself in any release so satisfying to her soul. For here was this mess of a leatherneck of hers to be washed up first. So like him to get all dirty the moment her back was turned! The first thing he knew as he came to was the feel of a rough pink tongue cleaning his ears.

I saw them all next day. An ambling passer-by, I came upon two cots shoved together under an apple tree. Belle and her ravenous pups occupied one of these. On the other the young marine—a gas case, I think, but maybe his stupor was shell shock and perhaps he had merely had a crack on the head—was deep in a dreamless sleep. Before drifting off he had taken the comforting precaution to reach out one hand and close it tight on a silken ear.

Later that day he told me all about his dog. I doubt if I ever knew his name, but some quirk of memory makes me think his home was in West Philadelphia and that he had joined up with the marines when he came out of school.

I went my way before dark and never saw them again, nor ever heard tell what became of the boy and his dog. I never knew when, if ever, he was shipped back into the fight, nor where, if ever, those two met again. It is, you see, a story without an end, though there must be those here and there in this country who witnessed and could set down for us the chapter that has never been written.

I hope there was something prophetic in the closing paragraph of the anonymous account of Verdun Belle which appeared the next week in the A.E.F. newspaper, *The Stars and Stripes*. That paragraph was a benison which ran in this wise:

Before long they would have to ship him on to the evacuation hospital, on from there to the base hospital, on and on and on. It was not very clear to anyone how another separation could be prevented. It was a perplexing question, but they knew in their hearts they could safely leave the answer to someone else. They could leave it to Verdun Belle.

Rags

EDMUND VANCE COOKE

We called him "Rags," he was just a cur,
But twice, on the Western Line,
That little old bunch of faithful fur
Had offered his life for mine.

And all that he got was bones and bread,
Or the leavings of soldier grub,

But he'd give his heart for a pat on the head,
   Or a friendly tickle and rub.

And Rags got home with the regiment,
   And then, in the breaking away—
Well, whether they stole him, or whether he went,
   I am not prepared to say.

But we mustered out, some to beer and gruel,
   And some to sherry and shad,
And I went back to the Sawbone School,
   Where I still was an undergrad.

One day they took us budding M.D.s
   To one of those institutes
Where they demonstrate every new disease
   By means of bisected brutes.

They had one animal tacked and tied
   And slit like a full-dressed fish,
With his vitals pumping away inside
   As pleasant as one might wish.

I stopped to look like the rest, of course,
   And the beast's eyes leveled mine;
His short tail thumped with a feeble force,
   And he uttered a tender whine.

It was Rags, yes, Rags! who was martyred there,
   Who was quartered and crucified,
And he whined that whine which is doggish prayer
   And he licked my hand—and died.

And I was no better in part nor whole
   Than the gang I was found among,

And his innocent blood was on the soul
Which he blessed with his dying tongue.

Well! I've seen men go to courageous death
In the air, on sea, on land!
But only a dog would spend his breath
In a kiss for his murderer's hand.

And if there's no heaven for love like that,
For such four-legged fealty—well!
If I have any choice, I tell you that,
I'll take my chance in hell.

The Dog
EDGAR A. GUEST

I like a dog at my feet when I read,
Whatever his size or whatever his breed.
A dog now and then that will nuzzle my hand
As though I were the greatest of men in the land,
And trying to tell me it's pleasant to be
On such intimate terms with a fellow like me.

I like a dog at my side when I eat,
I like to give him a bit of my meat;
And though mother objects and insists it is bad
To let dogs in the dining room, still I am glad

To behold him stretched out on the floor by my chair.
It's cheering to see such a faithful friend there.

A dog leads a curious life at the best.
By the wag of his tail is his pleasure expressed.
He pays a high tribute to man when he stays
True to his friend to the end of his days.
And I wonder sometimes if it happens to be
That dogs pay no heed of the faults which men see.

Should I prove a failure; should I stoop to wrong;
Be weak at a time when I should have been strong,
Should I lose my money, the gossips would sneer
And fill with my blundering many an ear,
But still, as I opened my door, I should see
My dog wag his tail with a welcome for me.

The Whistle

HUGH WALPOLE

Mrs. Penwin gave one of her nervous little screams when she saw the dog.

"Oh Charlie!" she cried. "You surely haven't bought it!" And her little nose, that she tried so fiercely to keep smooth, wrinkled into its customary little guttering of wrinkles.

The dog, taking an instant dislike to her, slunk, his head between his shoulders. He was an Alsatian.

"Well—" said Charlie, smiling nervously. He knew that his impulsiveness had led him once more astray. "Only the other evening you were saying that you'd like another dog."

"Yes, but *not* an Alsatian! You *know* what Alsatians are. We read about them in the paper every day. They are simply *not* to be trusted. I'm sure he looks as vicious as anything. And what about Mopsa?"

"Oh, Mopsa—" Charlie hesitated. "He'll be all right. You see, Sibyl, it was charity really. The Sillons are going to London as you know. They simply can't take him—it wouldn't be fair. They've found it difficult enough in Edinburgh as it is."

"I'm sure they are simply getting rid of him because he's vicious."

"No. Maude Sillon assured me he's like a lamb—"

"Oh, Maude! She'd say anything!"

"You know that you've been wanting a companion for Mopsa—"

"A companion for Mopsa! That's good!" Sibyl laughed her shrill little laugh that was always just out of tune.

"Well, we'll try him. We can easily get rid of him. And Blake shall look after him."

"Blake?" She was scornful. She detested Blake, but he was too good a chauffeur to lose.

"And he's most awfully handsome. You can't deny it."

She looked. Yes, he was most awfully handsome. He had laid down his head on his paws, staring in front of him, quite motionless. He seemed to be waiting scornfully until he should be given his next command. The power in those muscles, moulded under the skin, must be terrific. His long wolf ears lay flat. His color was lovely, here silver gray, there faintly amber. Yes, he was a magnificent dog. A little like Blake in his strength, silence, sulkiness.

She turned again to the note that she was writing.

"We'll try him if you like. Anyway there are no children about. It's Blake's responsibility—and the moment he's tiresome he goes."

Charlie was relieved. It hadn't been so hard after all.

"Oh, Blake says he doesn't mind. In fact he seemed to take to the dog at once. I'll call him."

He went to the double windows that opened into the garden and called: "Blake! Blake!" Blake came. He was still in his chauffeur's uniform, having just driven his master and the dog in from Keswick. He was a very large man, very fair in coloring, plainly of great strength. His expression was absolutely English in its complete absence of curiosity, its certainty that it knew the best about everything, its suspicion, its determination not to be taken in by anybody, and its latent kindliness. He had very blue eyes and was clean-shaven; his cap was in his hand and his hair, which was fair almost to whiteness, lay roughly across his forehead. He was not especially neat but of a quite shining cleanliness.

The dog got up and moved towards him. Both the Penwins were short and slight; they looked now rather absurdly small beside the man and the dog.

"Look here, Blake," said Charlie Penwin, speaking with much authority, "Mrs. Penwin is nervous about the dog. He's your responsibility, mind, and if there's the slightest bit of trouble, he goes. You understand that?"

"Yes, sir," said Blake, looking at the dog, "but there won't be no trouble."

"That's a ridiculous thing to say," remarked Mrs. Penwin sharply, looking up from her note. "How can you be sure, Blake? You know how uncertain Alsatians are. I don't know what Mr. Penwin was thinking about."

Blake said nothing. Once again, and for the hundred-thousandth time, both the Penwins wished that they could pierce him with needles. It was quite terrible the way that Blake didn't speak when expected to, but then he was so wonderful a chauffeur, so good a driver, so excellent a mechanic, so honest—and Clara, his wife, was an admirable cook.

"You'd better take the dog with you now, Blake. What's its name?"

"Adam," said Charlie.

"Adam! What a foolish name for a dog! Now don't disturb Clara with him, Blake. Clara hates to have her kitchen messed up."

Blake, without a word, turned and went, the dog following closely at his heels.

Yes, Clara hated to have her kitchen messed up. She was standing now, her sleeves rolled back, her plump hands and wrists covered with dough. Mopsa, the Sealyham, sat at her side, his eyes, glistening with greed, raised to those doughy arms. But at sight of the Alsatian he turned and flew at his throat. He was a dog who prided himself on fighting instantly every other dog. With human beings he was mild and indifferently amiable. Children could do what they would with him. He was exceedingly conceited, and cared for no one but himself.

He was clever, however, and hid this indifference from many sentimental human beings.

Blake, with difficulty, separated the two dogs. The Alsatian behaved quite admirably, merely noticing the Sealyham and looking up at Blake to say, "I won't let myself go here although I should like to. I know that you would rather I didn't." The Sealyham, muttering deeply, bore the Alsatian no grudge. He was simply determined that he should have no foothold here.

Torrents of words passed from Clara. She had always as much to say as her husband had little. She said the same thing many times over as though she had an idiot to deal with. She knew that her husband was not an idiot—very far from it—but she had for many years been trying to make some impression on him. Defeated beyond hope, all she could now do was to resort to old and familiar tactics. What was this great savage dog? Where had he come from? Surely the Mistress didn't approve, and she wouldn't have her kitchen messed up, not for anybody, and as Harry (Blake) very well knew, nothing upset her like a dog fight, and if they were going to be perpetual, which, knowing Mopsa's character, they probably would be, she must just go to Mrs. Penwin and tell her that, sorry though she was after being with her all these years, she just couldn't stand it and would have to go, for if there was one thing more than another that really upset her it was a dog fight, and as Harry knew having the kitchen messed up was a thing that she couldn't stand. She paused and began vehemently to roll her dough. She was short and plump with fair hair and blue eyes like her husband's.

When she was excited, little glistening beads of sweat appeared on her forehead. No one in this world knew whether Blake was fond of her or no, Clara Blake least of all. She wondered perpetually; this uncertainty and her cooking were her principal interests in life. There were times when Blake seemed very fond of her indeed, others when he appeared not to be aware that she existed.

All he said now was, "The dog won't be no trouble," and went out, the dog at his heels. The Sealyham thought for a moment that he would follow him, then, with a little sniff of greed, settled himself down again at Clara Blake's feet.

The two went out into the thin, misty autumn sunshine, down through the garden into the garage. The Alsatian walked very closely beside Blake as though some invisible cord held them together. All his life, now two years in length, it had been always his constant principle to attach himself to somebody. For, in this curious world where he was, not his natural world at all, every breath, every movement, rustle of wind, sound of voices, patter of rain, ringing of bells, filled him with nervous alarm. He went always on guard, keeping his secret soul to himself, surrendering nothing, a captive in the country of the enemy. There might exist a human being to whom he would surrender himself. Although he had been attached to several people, he had not in his two years yet found one to whom he could give himself. Now as he trod softly over the amber and rosy leaves he was not sure that this man, beside whom he walked, might not be the one.

In the garage Blake took off his coat, put on his blue overalls and began to work. The dog stretched himself out on the stone floor, his head on his paws, and waited. Once and again he started, his pointed ears pricked, at some unexpected sound. A breeze blew the brown leaves up and down in the sun, and the white road beyond the garage pierced like a shining bone the cloudless sky.

Blake's thoughts ran, as they always did, with slow assurance. This was a fine dog. He'd known the first moment that he set eyes on him that this was the dog for him. At that first glance something in his heart had been satisfied, something that had for years been unfulfilled. For they had had no children, he and Clara, and a motor car was fine to drive and look after, but after all it couldn't give you everything, and he wasn't one to make friends (too damned cautious), and the people he worked for were all right but nothing extra, and he really didn't know whether he cared for Clara or no. It was so difficult after so many years married to tell. There were lots of times when he couldn't sort of see her at all.

He began to take out the spark plugs to clean them. That was the worst of these Daimlers, fine cars, as good as any going, but you had to be forever cleaning the spark plugs. Yes, that dog was a beauty. He was going to take to that dog.

The dog looked at him, stared at him as though he were saying something. Blake looked at the dog. Then, with a deep sigh, as though some matter, for long uncertain, was at last completely settled, the dog rested again his head on his paws, staring in front of him, and so fell asleep. Blake, softly whistling, continued his work.

A very small factor, in itself quite unimportant, can bring into serious conflict urgent forces. So it was now when this dog, Adam, came into the life of the Penwins.

Mrs. Penwin, like so many English wives and unlike all American wives, had never known so much domestic power as she descried. Her husband was, of course, devoted to her, but he was forever just escaping her, escaping her into that world of men that is so important in England, that is, even in these very modern days, still a world in the main apart from women.

Charlie Penwin had not very many opportunities to escape from his wife, and he was glad that he had not, for when they came he took them. His ideal was the ideal of most English married men (and of very few American married men), namely, that he should be a perfect companion to his wife. He fulfilled this ideal; they were excellent companions, the two of them, so excellent that it was all the more interesting and invigorating when he could go away for a time and be a companion to someone else, to Willie Shaftoe, for instance, with whom he sometimes stayed in his place near Carlisle, or even for a few days' golf with the Reverend Thomas Bird, rector of a church in Keswick.

Mrs. Penwin in fact had nerves quite in spite of his profound devotion to her, never entirely captured the whole of her husband— a small fragment eternally escaped her, and this escape was a very real grievance to her. Like a wise woman she did not make scenes—no English husband can endure scenes—but she was always attempting to stop up this one little avenue of escape. But most provoking! So soon as one avenue was closed another would appear.

She realized very quickly (for she was not at all a fool) that this Alsatian was assisting her husband to escape from her because his presence in their household was bringing him into closer contact with Blake. Both the Penwins feared Blake had admired him; to friends and strangers they spoke of him with intense pride. "What we should do without Blake I can't think!" "But aren't we lucky in *these* days to have a chauffeur whom we can completely trust?"

Nevertheless, behind these sentiments there was this great difference, that Mrs. Penwin disliked Blake extremely (whenever he looked at her he made her feel a weak, helpless, and idiotic woman) while Charlie Penwin, although he was afraid of him, in his heart liked him very much indeed.

If Blake only were human, little Charlie Penwin, who was a sentimentalist, used to think—and now suddenly Blake *was* human. He had gone "dotty" about this dog, and the dog followed him like a shadow. So close were they the one to the other that you could almost imagine that they held conversations together.

Then Blake came into his master's room one day to ask whether Adam could sleep in his room. He had a small room next to Mrs. Blake's because he was often out late with the car at night or must rise very early in the morning. Clara Blake liked to have her sleep undisturbed.

"You see, sir," he said, "he won't sort of settle down in the outhouse. He's restless. I know he is."

"How do you know he is?" asked Charlie Penwin.

"I can sort of feel it, sir. He won't be no sort of trouble in my room, and he'll be a fine guard to the house at night."

The two men looked at one another and were in that moment friends. They both smiled.

"Very well, Blake. I don't think there's anything against it."

Of course, there *were* things against it. Mrs. Penwin hated the idea of the dog sleeping in the house. She did not really hate it; what she hated was that Blake and her husband should settle this thing without a word to her. Nor, when she protested, would her husband falter. Blake wanted it. It would be a good protection for the house.

Blake developed a very odd whistle with which he called the

dog. Putting his fingers into his mouth he called forth this strange melancholy note that seemed to penetrate into endless distance and that had in it something mysterious, melancholy, and dangerous. It was musical and inhuman; friends of the Penwins, comfortably at tea, would hear this thin whistling cry, coming, it seemed, from far away beyond the fells, having in it some part of the lake and the distant sea trembling on Drigg sands and of the lonely places in Eskdale and Ennerdale.

"What's that?" they would say, looking up.

"Oh, it's Blake calling the dog."

"What a strange whistle!"

"Yes, it's the only one the dog hears."

The dog did hear it, at any distance, in any place. When Blake went with the car the Alsatian would lie on the upper lawn whence he could see the road and wait for his return.

He would both see and hear the car's return, but he would not stir until Blake, released from his official duties, could whistle to him—then with one bound he would be up, down the garden, and with his front paws up against Blake's chest would show him his joy.

To all the rest of the world he was indifferent. But he was not hostile. He showed indeed an immense patience, and especially with regard to the Sealyham.

The dog Mopsa attempted twice at least every day to kill the Alsatian. He succeeded in biting him severely but so long as Blake was there he showed an infinite control, letting Blake part them although every instinct in him was stirred to battle.

But after a time, Blake became clever at keeping the two dogs separate; moreover, the Sealyham became afraid of Blake. He was clever enough to realize that when he fought the Alsatian he fought Blake as well—and Blake was too much for him.

Very soon, however, Blake was at war not only with the Sealyham but with his wife and Mrs. Penwin too. You might think that the words "at war" were too strong when nothing was to be seen on the surface. Mrs. Blake said nothing, Mrs. Penwin said nothing, Blake himself said nothing.

Save for the fights with the Sealyham, there was no charge

whatever to bring against the Alsatian. He was never in anyone's way, he brought no dirt in the house; whenever Charlie Penwin took him in the car he sat motionless on the back seat, his wolf ears pricked up, his large and beautiful eyes sternly regarding the outside world, but his consciousness fixed only upon Blake's back, broad and masterly above the wheel.

No charge could be brought against him except that the devotion between the man and the dog was in this little house of ordered emotions, routine habits, quiet sterility, almost terrible. Mrs. Blake, as her husband left her one night to return to his own room, broke out: "If you'd loved me as you love that dog I'd have had a different life."

Blake patted her shoulder, moist beneath her nightdress. "I love you all right, my girl," he said.

And Mrs. Penwin found that here she could not move her husband. Again and again she said: "Charlie, that dog's got to go."

"Why?"

"It's dangerous."

"I don't see it."

"Somebody will be bitten one day, and then you *will* see it."

"There's a terrible lot of nonsense talked about Alsatians—"

And then, when everyone was comfortable, Mrs. Blake reading her "Home Chat," Mrs. Penwin her novel, Mrs. Fern (Mrs. Penwin's best friend) doing a "cross-word," over the misty, dank garden, carried it seemed by the muffled clouds that floated above the fell, would sound that strange melancholy whistle, so distant and yet so near, Blake calling his dog.

For Blake himself life was suddenly, and for the first time, complete. He had not known, all this while, what it was that he missed although he had known that he missed something. Had Mrs. Blake given him a child he would have realized completion. Mrs. Blake alone had not been enough for his heart. In this dog he found fulfillment because here were all the things that he admired—loyalty, strength, courage, self-reliance, fidelity, comradeship, and, above all, sobriety of speech and behavior. Beyond these there was something more—love. He did not, even to himself, admit the significance of this yet deeper contact. And he analyzed nothing.

For the dog, life in this dangerous menacing country of the enemy was at last secure and simple. He had only one thing to do, only one person to consider.

But, of course, life is not so simple as this for anybody. A battle was being waged, and it must have an issue.

The Penwins were not in Cumberland during the winter. They went to their little place in Sussex, very close to London and to all their London friends. Mrs. Penwin would not take the Alsatian to Sussex. "But why not?" asked Charlie. She hated it, Mrs. Blake hated it. That, Charlie objected, was not reason enough.

"Do you realize," said Mrs. Penwin theatrically, "that this dog is dividing us?"

"Nonsense," said Charlie.

"It is not nonsense. I believe you care more for Blake than you do for me." She cried. She cried very seldom. Charlie Penwin was uncomfortable but some deep male obstinacy was roused in him. This had become an affair of the sexes. Men must stand together and protect themselves or they would be swept away in this feminine flood.

Blake knew, Mrs. Blake knew, Mrs. Penwin knew that the dog would go with them to Sussex unless some definite catastrophe gave Mrs. Penwin the victory.

Lying on his bed at night, seeing the gray wolf-like shadow of the dog stretched on the floor, Blake's soul for the first time in its history trembled, at the thought of the slight movement, incident, spoken word, sound that might rouse the dog beyond his endurance and precipitate the catastrophe. The dog was behaving magnificently, but he was surrounded by his enemies. Did he know what hung upon his restraint?

Whether he knew or no, the catastrophe arrived and arrived with the utmost, most violent publicity. On a sun-gleaming, russet October afternoon, on the lawn while Charlie was giving Blake instructions about the car and Mrs. Penwin put in also her word, Mopsa attacked the Alsatian. Blake ran to separate them, and the Alsatian, sharply bitten, bewildered, humiliated, snapped and caught Blake's leg between his teeth. A moment later he and Blake knew, both of them, what he had done. Blake would have hidden it, but blood was flowing. In the Alsatian's heart remorse, terror, love, and a sense of disaster—a confirmation of all that, since his birth, knowing the traps that his enemies would lay for him, he had suspected—leapt to life together.

Disregarding all else, he looked up at Blake.

"And that settles it!" cried Mrs. Penwin, triumphantly. "He goes!"

Blake's leg was badly bitten in three places; there would be scars for life. And it was settled. Before the week was out the dog would be returned to his first owners, who did not want him—who would give him to someone else who also, in turn, through fear or shyness of neighbors, would not want him.

Two days after this catastrophe, Mrs. Blake went herself to Mrs. Penwin.

"My husband's that upset—I wouldn't care if the dog stays, Mum."

"Why, Clara, you hate the dog."

"Oh well, Mum, Blake's a good husband to me. I don't like to see him—"

"Why, what has he said?"

"He hasn't said *anything*, Mum."

But Mrs. Penwin shook her head. "No, Clara, it's ridiculous. The dog's dangerous."

And Blake went to Charlie Penwin. The two men faced one another and were closer together, fonder of one another, man caring for man, than they had ever been before.

"But, Blake, if the dog bites *you* whom he cares for—I mean, don't you see? he really *is* dangerous—"

"He wasn't after biting me," said Blake slowly. "And if he *had* to bite somebody, being aggravated and nervous, he'd not find anyone better to bite than me who understands him and knows he don't mean nothing by it."

Charlie Penwin felt in himself a terrible disloyalty to his wife. She could go to— Why should not Blake have his dog? Was he forever to be dominated by women? For a brief rocking, threatening moment his whole ordered world trembled. He knew that if he said the dog was to remain the dog would remain and that something would have broken between his wife and himself that could never be mended.

He looked at Blake, who with his blue serious eyes stared steadily in front of him. He hesitated. He shook his head.

"No, Blake, it won't do. Mrs. Penwin will never be easy now while the dog is here."

Later in the day Blake did an amazing thing. He went to Mrs. Penwin.

During all these years he had never voluntarily, himself, gone to Mrs. Penwin. He had never gone unless he was sent for. She looked at him and felt, as she always did, dislike, admiration, and herself a bit of a fool.

"Well, Blake?"

"If the dog stays I'll make myself responsible. He shan't bite nobody again."

"But how can you tell? You said he wouldn't bite anyone before and he did."

"He won't again."

"No, Blake, he's got to go. I shan't have a moment's peace while he's here."

"He's a wonderful dog. I'll have him trained so he won't hurt a fly. He's like a child with me."

"I'm sure he is. Irresponsible like a child. That's why he bit you."

"I don't make nothing of his biting me."

"You may not, but next time it will be someone else. There's something in the paper about them every day."

"He's like a child with me."

"I'm very sorry, Blake. I can't give way about it. You'll see I'm right in the end. My husband ought never to have accepted the dog at all."

After Blake had gone she did not know why, but she felt uneasy, as though she had robbed a blind man, or stolen another woman's lover. Ridiculous! There could be no question but that she was right.

Blake admitted that to himself. She was right. He did not criticise her, but he did not know what to do. He had never felt like this in all his life before, as though part of himself were being torn from him.

On the day before the dog was to go back to his original owners Blake was sent into Keswick to make some purchases. It was a

soft blooming day, one of those North English autumn days when
there is a scent of spices in the sharp air and a rosy light hangs
about the trees. Blake had taken the dog with him, and driving
back along the lake, seeing how it lay, a sheet of silver glass upon
whose surface the islands were painted in flat colors of auburn
and smoky gray, a sudden madness seized him. It was the stillness,
the silence, the breathless pause—

Instead of turning to the right over the Grange bridge, he drove
the car straight on into Borrowdale. It was yet early in the afternoon—all the lovely valley lay in gold leaf at the feet of the russet
hills, and no cloud moved in the sky. He took the car to Seatoller
and climbed with the dog the steep path towards Honister.

And the dog thought that at last what he had longed for was
to come to pass. He and Blake were at length free, they would
go on and on, leaving all the stupid, nerve-jumping world behind
them, never to return to it.

With a wild, fierce happiness such as he had never yet shown
he bounded forward, drinking in the cold streams, feeling the
strong turf beneath his feet, running back to Blake to assure him
of his comradeship. At last he was free, and life was noble as it
ought to be.

At the turn of the road Blake sat down and looked back. All
around him were hills. Nothing moved; only the stream close to
him slipped murmuring between the boulders. The hills ran ranging
from horizon to horizon, and between gray clouds a silver strip
of sky, lit by an invisible sun, ran like a river into mist. Blake
called the dog to him and laid his hand upon his head. He knew
that the dog thought that they both had escaped forever now
from the world. Well, why not? They could walk on, on to the
foot of the hill on whose skyline the mining hut stood like a listening
ear, down the Pass to Buttermere, past the lake, past Crummock
Water to Cockermouth. There would be a train. It would not be
difficult for him to get work. His knowledge of cars (he had a
genius for them) would serve him anywhere. And Clara? She was
almost invisible, a tiny white blot on the horizon. She would find
someone else. His hand tightened about the dog's head.

For a long while he sat there, the dog never moving, the silver river spreading in the sky, the hills gathering closer about him.

Suddenly he shook his head. No, he could not. He would be running away, a poor kind of cowardice. He pulled Adam's sharp ears; he buried his face in Adam's fur. He stood up, and Adam also stood up, placed his paws on Blake's chest, licked his cheeks. In his eyes there shone great happiness because they two were going alone together.

But Blake turned back down the path, and the dog realizing that there was to be no freedom, walked close behind him, brushing with his body sometimes the stuff of Blake's trousers.

Next day Blake took the dog back to the place whence he had come.

Two days later, the dog, knowing that he was not wanted, sat watching a little girl who played some foolish game near him. She had plump bare legs; he watched them angrily. He was unhappy, lonely, nervous, once more in the land of the enemy, and now with no friend.

Through the air, mingling with the silly laughter of the child and other dangerous sounds came, he thought, a whistle. His heart hammered. His ears were up. With all his strength he bounded towards the sound. But he was chained. Tomorrow he was to be given to a Cumberland farmer.

Mrs. Penwin was entertaining two ladies at tea. This was the last day before the journey south. Across the dank lawns came that irritating, melancholy whistle disturbing her, reproaching her—and for what?

Why, for her sudden suspicion that everything in life was just ajar—one little push and all would be in its place—but would she be married to Charlie, would Mrs. Plang then be jealous of her pretty daughter, would Miss Tennyson, nibbling now at her pink pieces of icing, be nursing her aged and intemperate father? She looked up crossly.

"Really, Charlie, that must be Blake whistling. I can't think why now the dog's gone. To let us know what he thinks about it, I suppose." She turned to her friends, "Our chauffeur—a splendid man—we *are* so fortunate. Charlie, do tell him. It's such a hideous whistle anyway—and now the dog is gone—"

Bum

W. DAYTON WEDGEFARTH

He's a little dog, with a stubby tail,
    And a moth-eaten coat of tan,
And his legs are short, of the wabbly sort;
    I doubt if they ever ran;
And he howls at night, while in broad daylight
    He sleeps like a bloomin' log,
And he likes the food of the gutter breed;
    He's a most irregular dog.

I call him Bum, and in total sum
    He's all that his name implies,
For he's just a tramp with a highway stamp
    That culture cannot disguise;
And his friends, I've found, in the streets abound,
    Be they urchins or dogs or men;
Yet he sticks to me with a fiendish glee,
    It is truly beyond my ken.

I talk to him when I'm lonesome-like,
    And I'm sure that he understands
When he looks at me so attentively
    And gently licks my hands;
Then he rubs his nose on my tailored clothes,
    But I never say nought thereat,
For the good Lord knows I can buy more clothes,
    But never a friend like that!

A Poem for Little Dogs
NANCY BYRD TURNER

For all the faithful little dogs
That ever lived, no matter where,
I make a simple song today
  And fling it on the air,—

For little dogs too small to hunt,
Or guide, or guard their man's possessions,
Or do enormous deeds,—too small,
  In fact, to have professions;

Who never had a chance for fame,
And never could their fealty prove
By doing any single thing
  But love, and love, and love!

To all those little eager dogs
Of any place and any time
Who gave their best with might and main,
  I dedicate this rhyme!

How The Friendship Grew
ARTHUR FREDERICK JONES
JOHN RENDEL

It seems to have been in the Old Stone Age, about 25,000 or 30,000 years ago, that man and dog first struck up their abiding friendship. This is, of course, an archaeological guess, not a certainty, but it is a reasonable one. Mostly it is inferred from the recovery of doglike bone fragments and teeth from ancient burial grounds, kitchen middens, lake dwelling sites, and other rubbish and ruination which mark the presence of early man.

It is anybody's guess how the friendship developed in those dim beginnings when glaciers still advanced and retreated, creating the fresh contours of a virgin world. Perhaps initially it was a relationship based on utility. Dog always has been a good hunter and man was not then a notably efficient one. In any event, mutual liking and mutual advantage presumably were acknowledged, and thereafter Cro-Magnon man ventured forth for food with the first domestic animal trotting at his heels or snuffling a rabbit track up ahead.

So, through the centuries the two have gone together, man becoming an evermore accomplished hunter, and dog evolving with astonishing versatility into scores of breeds and acquiring many temperaments and functions. Dogs have been bred to point, flush, course, harry, unearth, and retrieve furred and feathered game. They have become specialists in bringing to bay the deer, elk, boar, otter, badger, fox, wolf, bear, antelope, lion and—the tapestries tell us—the unicorn. They are excellent sheepherders, the scourge of rats and rabbits, and the trusty sentinel of house and home. They are movie stars, military messengers, guides for the blind, and astronauts.

And they are pets. In all the wide earth there is no other creature—including other men—with whom man has lived so peaceably and successfully, or on whom he has lavished such loyalty, affection, and respect. Possibly, this is because dogs at their best embody many of the virtues man admires most in himself: patience, courage, obedience, tolerance, enthusiasm, humor, devotion. They are gentle, companionable, and confidential with children. They are gallant with women. And not a few men are the better for having had to live up to their dog's estimation of them.

Zoologically speaking, the dog is *canis familiaris*, a member of the *canidae* group of carnivores, which makes him a cousin of the wolf, the fox, and the jackal. The many evolutionary stages through which he has passed seem to have begun some 40,000,000 to 60,000,000 years ago with a weasel-like creature called Miacis, the paterfamilias from whom is descended the bear, raccoon, hyena, civet, and today's domestic cat. The most nearly doglike of the dog's ancestors probably was Cynodictus, a slender-bodied, short-legged animal about the size of a fox, that is considered to be a direct forebear of the dogs we know today.

What breed, then, was the first dog to make his way with man? No one knows, although very possibly by that time Cynodictus and his descendants had evolved into the great "parental" dogs from which so many of our contemporary purebreds have sprung. On the continent of Europe this might have been a Spitz type, the stocky, sharp-featured, bushy-tailed fellow with the handsome neck ruff, who is perpetuated today in the Norwegian Elkhound, Chow Chow, Samoyed, Keeshond, Pomeranian, and Siberian Husky. In the Middle East it would very likely have been the Saluki, the probable progenitor of the Greyhound, the Afghan, and the Borzoi. In Asia it could well have been the Tibetan mastiff, a dog still in existence, whose characteristics have long since become part of our big, blunt-muzzled, foursquare dogs, such as the Boxer, Bulldog, Great Dane, Rottweiler, St. Bernard, Great Pyrenees, and Newfoundland.

The Power of the Dog
RUDYARD KIPLING

There is sorrow enough in the natural way
From men and women to fill our day;
And when we are certain of sorrow in store,
Why do we always arrange for more?
*Brothers and Sisters, I bid you beware
Of giving your heart to a dog to tear.*

Buy a pup and your money will buy
Love unflinching that cannot lie—
Perfect passion and worship fed
By a kick in the ribs or a pat on the head.
*Nevertheless it is hardly fair
To risk your heart for a dog to tear.*

When the fourteen years which Nature permits
Are closing in asthma, or tumour, or fits,
And the vet's unspoken prescription runs
To lethal chambers or loaded guns,
*Then you will find—it's your own affair—
But . . . you've given your heart to a dog to tear.*

When the body that lived at your single will,
With its whimper of welcome, is stilled (how still!);
When the spirit that answered your every mood
Is gone—wherever it goes—for good,

You will discover how much you care,
And will give your heart to a dog to tear.

We've sorrow enough in the natural way,
When it comes to burying Christian clay.
Our loves are not given, but only lent,
At compound interest of cent per cent.
Though it is not always the case, I believe,
That the longer we've kept'em, the more do we grieve:
For, when debts are payable, right or wrong,
A short-time loan is as bad as a long—
So why in Heaven (before we are there)
Should we give our hearts to a dog to tear?

My Dog

MARTY HALE

A timid cringing little thing,
Bones coming through your hide—
I took your small nose in my hand,
You snuggled to my side;
You lifted soft dark eyes to me,
That told so silently
Of cold and hunger and abuse,
A stray dog's misery.
Fate might have been a bit to blame,
For I was lonely, too—
I needed just the sort of friend

I've always found in you.
When funny quirks of human friends
My mental lights befog,
I slip away a bit, alone,
And snuggle up my dog.

Snapshot of a Dog

JAMES THURBER

I ran across a dim photograph of him the other day. He's been dead 25 years. His name was Rex (my two brothers and I named him) and he was a bull terrier. "An American bull terrier," we used to say, proudly; none of your English bulls. He had one brindle eye that sometimes made him look like a clown and sometimes reminded you of a politician with derby hat and cigar. The rest of him was white except for a brindle saddle and a brindle stocking on a hind leg. Nevertheless, there was a nobility about him. He was big and muscular and beautifully made. He never lost his dignity even when trying to accomplish the extravagant tasks my brother and I used to set for him.

One of these was the bringing of a ten-foot wooden rail into the yard through the back gate. We would throw it out into the alley and tell him to get it. Rex was as powerful as a wrestler, and he would catch the rail at the balance, lift it clear of the ground, and trot with great confidence toward the gate. Of course, the gate being only four feet wide, he couldn't bring the rail in broadside. He found that out when he got a few terrific jolts, but he wouldn't give up. He finally figured out how to do it, by dragging the rail, holding onto one end, growling. He got a great, wagging satisfaction out of his work.

He was a tremendous fighter, but he never started fights. He never went for a dog's throat but for one of its ears (that teaches a dog a lesson), and he would get his grip, close his eyes, and hold on. He could hold on for hours. His longest fight lasted from dusk to almost pitch-dark, one Sunday. It was fought with a large, snarly nondescript belonging to a large colored man. When Rex finally got his ear grip, the brief whirlwind of snarling turned to screeching. It was frightening to listen to and to watch. The Negro boldly picked the dogs up, swung them around his head, and finally let them fly like a hammer in a hammer throw, but although they landed ten feet away, with a great plump, Rex still held on. Working their way to the middle of the car tracks, two or three streetcars were held up by the fight. A motorman tried to pry Rex's jaws open with a switch rod; somebody lighted a stick and held it to Rex's tail but he paid no attention. Rex's joy of battle, when battle was joined, was almost tranquil. He had a kind of pleasant expression during fights, his eyes closed in what would have seemed to be sleep had it not been for the turmoil of the struggle. The Fire Department finally had to be sent for and a powerful stream of water turned on the dogs for several moments before Rex finally let go.

The story of that Homeric fight got all around town, and some of our relatives considered it a blot on the family name. They insisted that we get rid of Rex, but nobody could have made us give him up. We would have left town with him first. It would have been different, perhaps, if he had ever looked for trouble. But he had a gentle disposition. He never bit a person in the ten strenuous years that he lived, nor ever growled at anyone except prowlers.

Swimming was his favorite recreation. The first time he ever saw a body of water, he trotted nervously along the steep bank for a while, fell to barking wildly, and finally plunged in from a height of eight feet or more. I shall always remember that shining, virgin dive. Then he swam upstream and back just for the pleasure of it, like a man. It was fun to see him battle upstream against a stiff current, growling every foot of the way. He had as much fun in the water as any person I have ever known. You didn't have to throw a stick into the water to get him to go in. Of course, he would bring back a stick if you did throw one in. He would have brought back a piano if you had thrown one in.

That reminds me of the night he went a-roving in the light of the moon and brought back a small chest of drawers he had found somewhere—how far from the house nobody ever knew. There were no drawers in the chest when he got it home, and it wasn't a good one—just an old cheap piece abandoned on a trash heap. Still it was something he wanted, probably because it presented a nice problem in transportation. We first knew about his achievement when, deep in the night, we heard sounds as if two or three people were trying to tear the house down. We came downstairs and turned on the porch light. Rex was on the top step, trying to pull the thing up, but it had caught and he was just holding his own. I suppose he would have held his own until dawn if we hadn't helped him. Next day we carted the chest miles away and threw it out. If we had thrown it out nearby, he would have brought it home again, as a small token of his integrity in such matters.

There was in his world no such thing as the impossible. Even death couldn't beat him down. He died, it is true, but only, as one of his admirers said, after "straight-arming the death angel" for more than an hour. Late one afternoon he wandered home, too slowly and uncertainly to be the Rex that had trotted briskly homeward up our avenue for ten years. I think we all knew when he came through the gate that he was dying. He had apparently taken a terrible beating, probably from the owner of some dog he had got into a fight with. His head and body were scarred, and some of the brass studs of his heavy collar were sprung loose. He licked at our hands and, staggering, fell, but got up again. We could see that he was looking for someone. One of his three masters was not home. He did not get home for an hour. During that hour the bull terrier fought against death as he had fought against the cold, strong current of the creek. When the person he was waiting for did come through the gate, whistling, ceasing to whistle, Rex walked a few wabbly paces toward him, touched his hand with his muzzle, and fell down again. This time he didn't get up.

pete's holiday
don marquis

We found a hill all green with grass
and cool with clover bloom
where bees go booming as they pass
boom zoom boom

my master took me in the car
and high upon the hill
we lay and stared up at the clouds
until the day grew chill

and moths came floating from the sky
and shadows stroked the ground
and we lay still and stared and stared
and what do you think we found

we found a star between the clouds
upon the edge of night
but when i jumped and barked at it
it hid itself in fright

then we drove back to town again
with my head on his lap

it tires a dog to scare a star
and then he needs a nap

my master is the same as god
when he thumps with his hand
people bring up hamburg steaks
at any eating stand

a master let us go right now
and find another star
and eat another hamburg steak
at a refreshment bar

A Kid and His Dog

LEROY J. FLEURY

Honest, Mom, I didn't coax him.
  He sort of lagged along behind;
Honest, Mom, I think he likes me—
  If I keep him, you won't mind?

Look, his little tail keeps wagging;
  See how cute he cocks his ear;
Honest, Mom, don't think I'm bragging,
  But he seems to like it here.

Honest, Mom, he'd be so useful—
  He could help me with the chores.

I'll just bet he'd pull a wagon
   With groceries from the store.

Some youngsters have to be born salesmen,
   If they get their folks' consent
To keep a faithful dog companion
   (That was nature's real intent).

Yet many men who have succeeded,
   Who've kept climbing up and up,
Help to build the character needed
   While in youth they loved a pup.

The Dog
(As seen by the cat)
OLIVER HERFORD

The Dog is black or white or brown,
   And sometimes spotted like a clown.
He loves to make a foolish noise,
   And Human Company enjoys.

The Human People pat his head
   And teach him to pretend he's dead,
And beg, and fetch, and carry, too;
   Things that no well-bred Cat will do

At Human jokes, however stale,
   He jumps about and wags his tail,

And Human People clap their hands
  And think he really understands.

They say "Good Dog" to him. To us
  They say "Poor Puss," and make no fuss.
Why Dogs are "good" and Cats are "poor"
  I fail to understand, I'm sure.

To Someone very Good and Just,
  Who has proved worthy of her trust,
A Cat will *sometimes* condescend—
  The Dog is Everybody's friend!

Lost Dog

MARGARET E. SANGSTER

I saw a little dog today,
  And oh, that dog was lost;
He risked his anguished puppy life
  With every street he crossed.
He shrank away from outstretched hands,
  He winced at every hail—
Against the city's bigness he
  Looked very small and frail.

Distrust lay in his tortured eyes,
  His body shook with fright;
(I wondered when he'd eaten last—
  And where he'd slept at night!)

I whistled, and I followed him,
 And hoped that he might guess
That all my soul reached out to him,
 And offered friendliness!

So many times I have been lost,
 And lonely and afraid!
I followed through the crowded streets,
 I followed—and I prayed.
And then the God of little things,
 Who knows when sparrows fall,
Put trust into the puppy's heart
 And made him heed my call. . . .

A Letter to the Man
Who Killed My Dog

RICHARD JOSEPH

I hope you were going somewhere important when you drove so fast down Cross Highway across Bayberry Lane, on Tuesday night.

I hope that when you got there the time you saved by speeding meant something to you or somebody else.

Maybe we'd feel better if we could imagine that you were a doctor rushing to deliver a baby or ease somebody's pain. The life of our dog to shorten someone's suffering—that mightn't have been so bad.

But even though all we saw of you was the black shadow of your car and its jumping red tail lights as you roared down the road, we know too much about you to believe it.

You saw the dog, you stepped on your brakes, you felt the thump, you heard the yelp and then my wife's scream. Your reflexes are better than your heart and stronger than your courage—we know that—because you jumped on the gas again and got out of there as fast as your car could carry you.

Whoever you are, mister, and whatever you do for a living, we know you are a killer.

And in your hands, driving the way you drove on Tuesday night, your car is a murder weapon.

You didn't bother to look, so I'll tell you what the thump and the yelp were. They were Vicky, a six-month-old Basset puppy; white with brown and black markings. An aristocrat, with twelve champions among her forebears; but she clowned and she chased, and she loved people and kids and other dogs as much as any mongrel on earth.

I'm sorry you didn't stick around to see the job you did, though a dying dog by the side of the road isn't a very pretty sight. In less than two seconds you and that car of yours transformed a living being that had been beautiful, warm, clean, soft and loving into something dirty, ugly, broken and bloody. A poor shocked and mad thing that tried to sink its teeth into the hand it had nuzzled and licked all its life.

I hope to God that when you hit my dog you had for a moment the sick, dead feeling in the throat and down in the stomach that we have known ever since. And that you feel it whenever you think about speeding down a winding country road again.

Because the next time some eight-year-old boy might be wobbling along on his first bicycle. Or a very little one might wander out past the gate and into the road in the moment it takes a father to bend down to pull a weed out of the drive, the way my pup got away from me.

Or maybe you'll be really lucky again, and only kill another dog, and break the heart of another family.

A Prayer
for the Dogs of War

MRS. E. WORTHING

Oh God, in your highest glory
Forget not these silent ones.
They too, show a soldier's courage
In this time of sorrow and death.
They too, lose their homes and their loved ones.
They too, are blinded and maimed.
Oh God, in your highest glory do not forget!
Pity! We ask Thee! Pity!
For these dark beseeching eyes,
For this shattered paw—
For this one, so small,
Who met death from the screaming skies!
Oh God, in your highest glory
Forget not these silent ones;
They ask naught but to be with
Their loved ones, when peace again shall come.

If You Have a Dog
DOUGLAS MALLOCH

Loss may grieve you, love may leave you,
  Idle tongues may lie;
Luck may quit you, trouble hit you,
  Fame may pass you by;
Thorns may hurt you, men desert you,
  Sunlight turn to fog,
But you're never friendless ever,
  If you have a dog.

Storms may beat you, foes defeat you,
  Fortune treat you ill;
All your dreaming, all your scheming,
  All be dreaming still.
Hate may hate you, woe await you,
  Rock and root and bog,
Yet an endless friend and friendless
  If you have a dog.

Though a rover oceans over,
  Though the world you roam;
Whether valley, street or alley,
  You may call a home;
King or vassal, cave or castle,
  Or a house or log,

One will bear it, one will share it,
    If you have a dog.

Vines may trip you, branches grip you,
    Clouds may hide the morn;
Men may doubt you; all about you,
    Those you love may scorn;
Still unshaken, unmistaken,
    You will face the fog,
God believing, though you're grieving,
    If you have a dog.

The Dogs in My Life
ROGER CARAS

To try to reconstruct or comment on the history of man and dog and remain clinical about that historical interaction is a difficult task. Sentimentality has seeped through every crack, permeates every layer of fabric; it runs as a theme throughout it all. As I think back over my own life I can view it as a chain of dogs and dog-related events, and each taught me a lesson, often about myself. There has been much more than dogs, of course—other animals, naturally, and people, marriage, children, career, sickness, travel, adventure, perhaps—but always dogs. They were always there, links from age to age, place to place, stage to stage. I am not sure I can even recall all of them by name, there have been that many.

The first dog of which I have any memory at all was a Boston

terrier and was on site before I was born. I don't know how long
he lasted, but I do remember him. He was the first dog I touched,
the first that ever licked me, but before I could judge the experience
he was gone. Certainly, though, the total experience was posi-
tive, for it was he who must have marked me with a very gentle
scar on my heart. A wire fox terrier (they were commonly called
wirehaired fox terriers then) was around for a long time;
that was Bozo. I believe I was about eight when he died. Not
long ago I went back to look at that house where the fox terrier
and I grew up together. It was strange. I felt he should still have
been there. That fox terrier taught me the meaning of faith and
loyalty.

The fox terrier was replaced by a collie puppy. That was to be
a short, sad event. I remember kneeling beside that collie in the
front yard as he lay dying. He was still a puppy, but he had
somehow gotten a chicken bone and it had ripped him up inside.
He was finally put down by a veterinarian, but he was almost
dead by that time. I learned about mortality from that puppy. It
was shocking to learn that the young could die, to come to know
how fragile it all is, especially life.

When my older brother was thirteen—that would have me about
eight and a half—Peter arrived. He was an English cocker spaniel,
all black with reddish-brown markings, perfectly balanced accents
over the eyes, on the cheeks, and on the legs. He was a magnificent
animal and was so close to human it was frightening. We moved
from the country town of Methuen, Massachusetts, to Boston while
we had Peter, and I remember the day he was hit by a car as he
rushed off our apartment-house lawn to greet me coming home
from school. He ran back onto the grass and promptly vomited.
Our family pediatrician was coming that day, and he examined
Peter's leg and splinted it. It probably wasn't even broken. As
long as Peter lived—and that was to a ripe old age, approaching
fifteen, as I recall—he would begin limping the moment he was
scolded or thought he was about to be. Otherwise, his leg was
fine. He never forgot the sympathy he had gotten while splinted,
and although I can't determine with exactitude what intelligence
is needed to develop a ruse like a fake limp, it seems to me it

must be considerable. I suppose it is always possible that it wasn't intelligence but something rather more Pavlovian than that. Still, I like to think he was a very clever dog.

I do remember this dog very clearly, because my teenage years were particularly rough ones. I could trust Peter as I could trust no one else, nothing else, then in my life. He listened and listened and listened. He slept with me, sat with me, walked with me, looked up to me, and never once judged. Everyone else did judge me, and not too favorably at that. Peter was an anchor I really don't know what I would have done without.

World War II came when Peter was about five years old and I was thirteen. My older brother went off to the army, and Peter became all mine. He was my constant companion until I went in the army myself and was still there when I was discharged and headed off for college. He finally died when I was in school far from Boston. That one little dog with his fake limp as needed seemed to span a major portion of my life. From well before I was ten through all of high school, the army, and much of my college career, that dog remained unchanging, always pleasant, always grateful for so much as a touch. Few people have had better friends than that. By the time Peter's life had run its course I was locked into dogs forever. I am not sure I ever had a choice.

The Dachshund

JOHN E. DONOVAN

A Dachshund sniffing round a tree
  Made such a wondrous bend, sir,
He filled himself with mystery—
  Not knowing his own end, sir.

Some other dogs have keener sight,
  And some have greater strength, sir,
But no dogs manage, for their height,
  To have so much of length, sir.

One time—at least, so people say—
  One lost his tail by train, sir;
Yet two weeks passed until the day
  The sad news reached his brain, sir.

The Dachshund looks a little bit
  Like legs beneath a log, sir,
But once your eyes get used to it,
  You see that it's a dog, sir.

My Airedale Dog

W. L. MASON

I have a funny Airedale dog,
　He's just about my size,
With such a serious-looking face,
　And eyes that seem so wise.

He looks as if he'd like to laugh,
　But yet his long, straight muzzle
Gives him a kind of solemn look—
　He surely is a puzzle.

And he is just as full of tricks
　As any dog could be,
And we have mighty jolly times
　Because he plays with me,

And never tries to bite or snap;
　He doesn't even whine,—
And that is why my Airedale dog
　Is such a friend of mine.

Keeper—Emily Brontë's Boxer
FAIRFAX DOWNEY

Never strike him or he will fly at your throat!"

Such was the warning with which the big tawny dog was given Emily Brontë, and he looked fully capable of murderous assault, if provoked. Part mastiff, part bulldog, Keeper was of the breed known today as Boxers. "His growl is more terrible than the bark, menacing as muted thunder," wrote his new mistress. Yet the gentle, fragile girl instantly took the grim, fierce creature to her heart, for she loved all animals, and a wild strain in them always appealed to her.

Keeper responded to her affection. For the rest of the world he cared nothing, but Emily was his idol. He strode at her heels in long walks across the moors and lay beside her on the rug when she read, her arm around his neck. At her command he would roar like a lion. She salved his wounds from fights with other dogs and mentioned him fondly in her letters. She painted his portrait in water-colors. Although Keeper does not appear in her novel, *Wuthering Heights*, he is the savage dog, "Tartar," in *Shirley* by her sister, Charlotte, and Emily is the heroine of that book, which followed Charlotte's classic *Jane Eyre*.

They made a strange pair, Keeper and the delicate Emily. The curate, paying a call, regarded them disapprovingly and observed that ladies generally liked lap dogs. Firmly Emily replied: "Perhaps I am an exception."

But an air of apprehension hung over the Brontë household. Keeper had a bad habit: he persisted in springing up and reposing on clean beds, and Emily vowed she would break him of it. None doubted she would try. A while ago she had given a pan of water to a slavering dog which wandered to the door. He proved to be rabid and sank his teeth in her hand. The girl ran to the fireplace, snatched out a red-hot poker, cauterized the bite and prevented infection. Yet punishing Keeper was a grave matter. That warning was fresh in everyone's mind. "Never strike him or he will fly at your throat."

The day came when Keeper was reported taking his ease on the best bed in the parsonage. In fear and trembling, the family watched Emily enter, pale but with her mouth set, her eyes blazing. She seized the big dog by the scruff of the neck and dragged him, growling ferociously, downstairs. In the corner behind the stairway, she released him and beat him again and again with small, clenched fists. Keeper stood, utterly stupefied, until his mistress led him away and weepingly bathed his bruises. He never bore her a grudge.

When she was only thirty, Emily, never strong, became fatally ill. On the last day of her life in 1848 she insisted on braving the December cold to feed Keeper as usual outdoors. That evening she died. Along with the family, the dog followed her coffin to the grave and sat quietly in the church through the service. Then he lay down outside the door of her bedroom, howling piteously. Until his death three years later, he visited the room daily to snuff and whine for his lost mistress.

"Let us somehow hope, in half Red Indian creed, that he follows Emily now," wrote Mrs. Gaskell, the Brontës' biographer, "and, when he rests, sleeps on some soft, white bed of dreams, unpunished when he awakens to the life of the land of shadows."

Raggles

ROBERT C. V. MEYERS

Says the Colonel to the sergeant, "I was kept awake all night
By that yellow cur of yours 'mong the trees."
Says the sergeant, "If you please, sir, your house was not shut
    tight—
Raggles barked at that, sir, if you please."

Says the Colonel, "All the same, put a shot in him
This evening before taps. That will do."
"All right sir," says the sergeant, touchin' his hat rim,
And the Colonel saunters off, frownin' too.

Then the sergeant goes to quarters, and there old Raggles lay,
Just a red, long-legged imp of a dog,
He was dreamin' of stray cats for his mouth just worked that way,
Though he slept on the floor like a log.

"Raggles!" says the sergeant, and Raggles wags his tail
And jumps up and licks the sergeant's hand.
"It's come at last, Raggles," says the sergeant—he was pale,
And Raggles somehow seemed to understand.

"Raggles," says the sergeant, "we've been friends many years.
You follered me from home, don't you know.
But the Colonel don't like you and sometimes it appears
You nip the foot that kicks you—yes, that's so.

"And last night you barked because the Colonel's door
Was carelessly left open, and you thought

A burglar wouldn't come if you barked all night, you cur,
And the Colonel couldn't sleep as he ought.

"But we've been good friends, Raggles; you remember what I
  do—
All the home folks, and old friends. But then
The Colonel couldn't sleep last night because of you
A-barkin' 'round his house. So to-night when—

"No, Raggles, I can't do it. Here, Bill!" he calls out
To the orderly, and told him what to do.
And the orderly led off Raggles, pullin' him about
With a rope 'round his neck,—pulled tight, too.

So the orderly tied up Raggles to the stump of a tree
Down by the creek where violets grew,
And left him there whinin' for the sergeant, for you see
Raggles loved the man, as dogs will do.

Well, the day passed along and the sergeant heard him bark,
Yet he did what he must, but paler grew
As the hours raced away; till just as it grew dark
He just fell a-tremblin', through and through.

And then he made a dash and got to the creek
And he hugged Raggles once, then was gone;
And Raggles just had time to give his face a lick—
And all the more he kept tuggin' on.

Then the sergeant went to quarters—he knew the boys would go
In a body to see Raggles get his dose—
And while waiting there, a whine, curious like and low
Sent his hands to his ears clappin' close.

He thought the orderly'd gone to Raggles by the creek
With his gun levelled ready for the crack,
And his heart gave a thump as though 'twas goin' to break—
For the world without Raggles would seem black.

He didn't want to hear when the bullet hit its mark,
And he thought of his home far away,

Where he used to get awake a-hearin' Raggles bark
And'd have him trottin' with him all the day.

But you see, when Raggles whined out there by the creek
When the first shadows fell, 'twas just this:
The Colonel's little daughter went violets to pick—
She was just the prettiest, daintiest little miss—

And she went too near the creek and overboard she fell,
And she cried a little bit, then was still;
'Twas then Raggles whined, there was nobody to tell,
And he tugged at his rope with a will.

He tugged till it choked him, his tongue hangin' out,
And his throat all a-bleedin'. But at last
The rope broke, and Raggles, tumblin' on his snout,
Like a flash of mangy lightnin' darted past.

He had the little missy before you could count ten,
And he ran with her to the Colonel's door,
And there he laid her drippin', he gaspin' by her, then
The boys who saw it they set up a roar.

The Colonel grabs his child, he couldn't speak at once,
Then he asked, "Where's the sergeant?" And they said
He was hidin' till old Raggles had been shot. And that dunce
Of an orderly said: "I've a bullet for his head."

Says the Colonel, "Shoot me first. Let the sergeant have his dog—
The dog watched my house, too, all last night,
And just now we've found a thief lyin' in the bog
Which the dog had punished bad in the fight.

"Tell the sergeant to come see me, and let him bring his dog
His dog? He's the regiment's instead."
And there stood the sergeant, his wits in a fog,
Though he'd heard every word the Colonel said.

But all at once he fell and caught Raggles by the head,
And he kissed him, Raggles lickin' off his tears.

"Give a cheer for the Colonel," the sergeant sobbin' said.
But the boys cried, "Cheer for Raggles. Give *three* cheers!"

Apology to a Small Dog
TEDDY WEBB

Little gray dog, don't run, don't fear,
This hurts me worse than you, my dear.
I am the one who fills the tub,
Who has to coax and soothe and scrub
And patiently endure each scratch,
Who, while you're rinsed, the showers catch.

There now, you're drying. Shake and sigh.
Comfort me with a martyred eye.
Soon you'll forget in rampant zest
A painful interlude at best,
Which was, forgive me, not in vain,
For little dog, you're white again.

Judy the Nurse Dog
JAMES HERRIOT

I first met Judy the Sheepdog when I was treating Eric's bullock for wooden tongue. The bullock was only a young one and the farmer admitted ruefully that he had neglected it because it was almost a walking skeleton.

"Damn!" Eric grunted. "He's been runnin' out with that bunch in the far fields and I must have missed 'im. I never knew he'd got to this state."

When actinobacillosis affects the tongue it should be treated right at the start, when the first symptoms of salivation and swelling beneath the jaw appear. Otherwise the tongue becomes harder and harder till finally it sticks out of the front of the mouth, as unyielding as the wood which gives the disease its ancient name.

This skinny little creature had reached that state, so that he not only looked pathetic but also slightly comic, as though he were making a derisive gesture at me. But with a tongue like that he just couldn't eat and was literally starving to death. He lay quietly as though he didn't care.

"There's one thing, Eric," I said. "Giving him an intravenous injection won't be any problem. He hasn't the strength to resist."

The great new treatment at that time was sodium iodide into the vein—modern and spectacular. Before that the farmers used to paint the tongue with tincture of iodine, a tedious procedure which sometimes worked and sometimes didn't. The sodium iodide was a magical improvement and showed results within a few days.

I inserted the needle into the jugular and tipped up the bottle of clear fluid. Two drachms of iodide I used to use, in eight ounces of distilled water, and it didn't take long to flow in. In fact the bottle was nearly empty before I noticed Judy.

I had been aware of a big dog sitting near me all the time, but as I neared the end of the injection a black nose moved ever closer till it was almost touching the needle. Then the nose moved along the rubber tube up to the bottle and back again, sniffing with the utmost concentration. When I removed the needle the nose began a careful inspection of the injection site. Then a tongue appeared and began to lick the bullock's neck methodically.

I squatted back on my heels and watched. This was something more than mere curiosity; everything in the dog's attitude suggested intense interest and concern.

"You know, Eric," I said, "I have the impression that this dog isn't just watching me. She's supervising the whole job."

The farmer laughed. "You're right there. She's a funny old bitch is Judy—sort of a nurse. If there's anything amiss she's on duty. You can't keep her away."

Judy looked up quickly at the sound of her name. She was a handsome animal; not the usual color, but a variegated brindle with waving lines of brown and grey mingling with the normal black and white of the farm collie. Maybe there was a cross somewhere, but the result was very attractive and the effect was heightened by her bright-eyed, laughing-mouthed friendliness.

I reached out and tickled the backs of her ears and she wagged mightily—not just her tail but her entire rear end. "I suppose she's just good-natured."

"Oh aye, she is," the farmer said. "But it's not only that. It sounds daft but I think Judy feels a sense of responsibility to all the stock on t'farm."

I nodded. "I believe you. Anyway, let's get this beast on to his chest."

We got down in the straw and with our hands under the back bone, rolled the bullock till he was resting on his sternum. We balanced him there with straw bales on either side, then covered him with a horse rug.

In that position he didn't look as moribund as before, but the emaciated head with the useless jutting tongue lolled feebly on his shoulders and the saliva drooled uncontrolled on to the straw. I wondered if I'd ever see him alive again.

Judy, however, didn't appear to share my pessimism. After a thorough sniffing examination of rug and bales she moved to the front, applied an encouraging tongue to the shaggy forehead, then stationed herself comfortably facing the bullock, very like a night nurse keeping an eye on her patient.

"Will she stay there?" I closed the half-door and took a last look inside.

"Aye, nothing'll shift her till he's dead or better," Eric replied. "She's in her element now."

"Well, you never know, she may give him an interest in life, just sitting there. He certainly needs some help. You must keep him alive with milk or gruel till the injection starts to work. If he'll drink it it'll do him most good, but otherwise you'll have to bottle it into him. But be careful—you can choke a beast that way."

A case like this had more than the usual share of the old fascination because I was using a therapeutic agent which really worked— something that didn't happen too often at that time. So I was eager to get back to see if I had been able to pull that bullock from the brink of death. But I knew I had to give the drug a chance and kept away for five days.

When I walked across the yard to the box I knew there would be no further doubts. He would either be dead or on the road to recovery.

The sound of my steps on the cobbles hadn't gone unnoticed. Judy's head, ears cocked, appeared above the half-door. A little well of triumph brimmed in me. If the nurse was still on duty then the patient must be alive. And I felt even more certain when the big dog disappeared for a second, then came soaring effortlessly over the door and capered up to me, working her hind end into convolutions of delight. She seemed to be doing her best to tell me all was well.

Inside the box the bullock was still lying down but he turned to look at me and I noticed a strand of hay hanging from his mouth. The tongue itself had disappeared behind the lips.

"Well, we're winning, aren't we?" Eric Abbot came in from the yard.

"Without a doubt," I said. "The tongue's much softer and I see he's been trying to eat hay."

"Aye, can't quite manage it yet, but he's suppin' the milk and gruel like a good 'un. He's been up a time or two but he's very wobbly on his pins."

I produced another bottle of sodium iodide and repeated the injection with Judy's nose again almost touching the needle as she sniffed avidly. Her eyes were focused on the injection site with fierce concentration and so intent was she on extracting the full savour that she occasionally blew out her nostrils with a sharp blast before recommencing her inspection.

When I had finished she took up her position at the head and as I prepared to leave I noticed a voluptuous swaying of her hips which were embedded in the straw. I was a little puzzled until I realized she was wagging in the sitting position.

"Well, Judy's happy at the way things are going," I said.

The farmer nodded. "Yes, she is. She likes to be in charge. Do you know, she gives every new-born calf a good lick over as soon as it comes into t'world and it's the same whenever one of our cats 'as kittens."

"Bit of a midwife, too, eh?"

"You could say that. And another funny thing about 'er—she lives with the livestock in the buildings. She's got a nice warm kennel but she never bothers with it—sleeps with the beasts in the straw every night."

I revisited the bullock a week later and this time he galloped round the box like a racehorse when I approached him. When I finally trapped him in a corner and caught his nose I was breathless but happy. I slipped my fingers into his mouth; the tongue was pliable and almost normal.

"One more shot, Eric," I said. "Wooden tongue is the very devil for recurring if you don't get it cleared up thoroughly." I began to unwind the rubber tube. "By the way, I don't see Judy around."

"Oh, I reckon she feels he's cured now, and anyway, she has summat else on her plate this mornin'. Can you see her over there?"

I looked through the doorway. Judy was stalking importantly across the yard. She had something in her mouth—a yellow, fluffy object.

I craned out further. "What is she carrying?"

"It's a chicken."

"A chicken?"

"Aye, there's a brood of them runnin' around just now. They're only a month old and t'awd bitch seems to think they'd be better off in the stable. She's made a bed for them in there and she keeps tryin' to curl herself round them. But the little things won't 'ave it."

I watched Judy disappear into the stable. Very soon she came out, trotted after a group of tiny chicks which were pecking happily among the cobbles and gently scooped one up. Busily she made her way back to the stable but as she entered, the previous chick reappeared in the doorway and pottered over to rejoin his friends.

She was having a frustrating time but I knew she would keep at it because that was the way she was.

Judy the nurse dog was still on duty.

The caring instinct in animals is manifested most obviously in the maternal feeling, surely one of the most powerful and most commonly observed characteristics, but Judy is the only animal I have ever known whose concern embraced all her fellow creatures. As Eric Abbot said, she was in her element when there was any sickness among his livestock. She was a natural canine nurse, and so unique in my experience that I have often wondered if anybody else has encountered one like her.

Epitaph to a Dog
LORD BYRON

On a monument in the garden of Newstead Abbey:

NEAR THIS SPOT
ARE DEPOSITED THE REMAINS
OF ONE
WHO POSSESSED BEAUTY
WITHOUT VANITY,
STRENGTH WITHOUT INSOLENCE,
COURAGE WITHOUT FEROCITY,
AND ALL THE VIRTUES OF MAN
WITHOUT HIS VICES.

THIS PRAISE, WHICH WOULD BE UNMEANING FLATTERY
IF INSCRIBED OVER HUMAN ASHES,
IS BUT A JUST TRIBUTE TO THE MEMORY OF
"BOATSWAIN," A DOG
WHO WAS BORN AT NEWFOUNDLAND,
MAY, 1803,
AND DIED AT NEWSTEAD ABBEY
NOV. 18, 1808

When some proud son of man returns to earth,
Unknown to glory, but upheld by birth,
The sculptor's art exhausts the pomp of woe,
And storied urns record who rests below;
When all is done, upon the tomb is seen,
Not what he was, but what he should have been.
But the poor dog, in life the firmest friend,
The first to welcome, foremost to defend,

Whose honest heart is still his master's own,
Who labors, fights, lives, breathes for him alone,
Unhonored falls, unnoticed all his worth,
Denied in heaven the soul he held on earth—
While man, vain insect! hopes to be forgiven,
And claims himself a sole exclusive heaven.

Oh man! thou feeble tenant of an hour,
Debased by slavery, or corrupt by power—
Who knows thee well must quit thee with disgust,
Degraded mass of animated dust!
Thy love is lust, they friendship all a cheat,
Thy smiles hypocrisy, they words deceit!
By nature vile, ennobled but by name,
Each kindred brute might bid thee blush for shame.
Ye, who perchance behold this simple urn,
Pass on—it honors none you wish to mourn.
To mark a friend's remains these stones arise;
I never knew but one—and there he lies.

The Duel

EUGENE FIELD

The gingham dog and the calico cat
Side by side on the table sat;
'Twas half-past twelve, and (what do you think!)
Nor one nor t'other had slept a wink!
  The old Dutch clock and the Chinese plate

Appeared to know as sure as fate
There was going to be a terrible spat.
  (I wasn't there; I simply state
  What was told to me by the Chinese plate!)

The gingham dog went "bow-wow-wow!"
And the calico cat replied "mee-ow!"
The air was littered, an hour or so,
With bits of gingham and calico,
  While the old Dutch clock in the chimney-place
  Up with its hands before its face,
For it always dreaded a family row!
  (Now mind: I'm only telling you
  What the old Dutch clock declares is true!)

The Chinese plate looked very blue,
And wailed, "Oh, Dear! what shall we do!"
But the gingham dog and the calico cat
Wallowed this way and tumbled that,
  Employing every tooth and claw
  In the awfullest way you ever saw—
And, oh! how the gingham and calico flew!
  (Don't fancy I exaggerate—
  I got my news from the Chinese plate!)

Next morning, where the two had sat
They found no trace of dog or cat;
And some folks think unto this day
That burglars stole that pair away!
  But the truth about the cat and pup
  Is this: they ate each other up!
Now what do you really think of that!
  (The old Dutch clock it told me so,
  And that is how I came to know.)

On Parting with Spot

HELEN WELSHIMER

Won't somebody please take care of Spot?
    I can't keep him any more.
My mother got cross at him because
    He tracked mud across the floor.
He's the nicest dog in the world, I guess;
    I love him an awful lot,
But I won't be seeing him any more.
    Please, someone, take care of Spot!

I'm putting a card around his neck,
    But it hasn't got room to say
How he won't let anyone strange come near
    Our house when we're all away.
He can carry a bag and find a ball
    And he's safe to play with and touch.
He's always slept by the side of my bed
    And he doesn't eat very much.

He's going to be lonesome just like me,
    But he wouldn't feel quite so bad,
If you pat his head—he's the grandest dog
    Almost that you ever had.
Maybe someone will read the sign
    Who's wanting a dog a lot,
And know that he is a reg'lar pup.
    Won't someone take care of Spot?

Gutsy

ROGER CARAS

When I was fourteen years old, and large for my age, I got a job at the famed Angell Memorial Animal Hospital. Located on Longwood Avenue in the heart of Boston's vast, sprawling medical district—Beth Israel, Boston Lying-in, Boston Children's, Harvard Medical School, Mass. Dental, and a host of other institutions were all within a few blocks of Angell—it has been consistently rated one of the finest veterinary hospitals in the world. It was operated then in its old setting and is today in its new home on South Huntington Avenue by the Massachusetts Society for the Prevention of Cruelty to Animals. The MSPCA is one of the oldest humane societies in the western hemisphere.

The first assignment given to the eager and somewhat brash new boy was, of course, cage cleaning. After my initial trial period I graduated to the waist-high bathtubs in the grooming section, watching my hands and forearms turn into prunes as I worked. I bathed, clipped, and deburred dogs all day long. I seriously questioned if my back would ever be right again. A slight forward tilt for eight hours a day can do one heck of a job, even on a teenager's sacroiliac.

Promotions came in proper order, and after passing through some less rewarding departments (like the euthanasia room) I ended up in white jacket in the clinic helping the staff veterinarians, or at least doing menial chores that made their lives a little easier. I hoisted animals on and off examining tables (after first lathering the stainless-steel surfaces with antiseptic solutions), held animals while they were examined and treated, guided clients in and out, and took dogs and cats back and logged them in if they had to be hospitalized. It was a rich experience for a boy just turning fifteen. Heading for work after school and on weekends didn't seem a chore, really. I was beginning to focus on a career. At that point I was determined to become a veterinarian.

One day the veterinarian on duty groaned as he pulled a card from the wooden holder on the wall. It was a familiar card, one side completely filled in with very little room left on the reverse.

"O.K., ask Mr. Jones to come in." (Jones was not his name, but that hardly matters.)

The client was a tired man with gray skin. He gave the impression that life had not been an unmixed blessing. His weariness hung on him like an ill-fitting shawl. In his arms, wrapped in an old but obviously frequently laundered blanket, was a positively ancient Boston terrier. The old man put his old dog on the table gently, obviously with love, and looked up at the tall young veterinarian, who towered over him. There was some hope in the old man's eyes, a little, but not really very much.

The veterinarian had seen this dog before, often, but he went through the gestures of examining him: stethoscope to heart, palpation of the abdomen, a look in the mouth and down the throat, a quick glance in the ears.

"The new medicine doesn't seem to be helping very much," the old man fairly croaked. "It's hard to tell, but there doesn't seem to be much change."

The veterinarian looked down at the floor for a moment, then put his foot on the rung of the examining table. He took a deep breath and leaned forward, prepared to make the speech he had made so many times before.

"You know there is never going to be any change, Mr. Jones. You know very well I am giving you medication for . . ." The veterinarian glanced over at the record card. ". . . for Gutsy to humor you. I can't be any blunter than that. Your dog is eighteen years old. He is blind, deaf, incontinent, he can't walk, he is frightened and in pain, and you are not being nice to him by keeping him alive this long. In nature he would have died long ago."

The young doctor was really being as kind as he knew how to

be, but he had been begging Mr. Jones to have his dog put to sleep for over six months. Mr. Jones, however, was back every week trying new medication, always with the faintest hint of hope in his eyes. We all knew him. We all understood his plight, or at least we thought we did. There wasn't a veterinarian or kennel helper at Angell who hadn't been through the same scene many times before.

"You don't think there is anything you can do?" The same question was asked every week.

"No, I *know* there is nothing we can do. We can't turn back the clock, and time has run out on Gutsy. You are not being kind to him by prolonging this very bad period for him."

The old man thought for a moment, then shook his head. He had come to a decision.

"Well, if it must be it must be. I'll take him home and do it now."

The veterinarian reached out and took the old man's elbow as he bent forward to wrap his old dog up and carry him away.

"Don't do that, please. It is a very difficult thing to do at home. You won't have the right materials, and you will be cruel to him even though you are trying to be kind. Let me do it here. I have a drug that will work very quickly. You can stay and help me if you want. You hold him and I will give him an injection. He won't even feel it and it will be over instantly. You will be able to see that for yourself. Please, don't try it yourself."

The old man thought again for a moment, then looked up into the veterinarian's eyes. Having finally decided to put his dog to death, the old man was finding new strengths, strengths that obviously had been eluding him for a long time.

"My wife died almost twenty years ago. I never wanted to remarry. We had just one son, and he married a girl in China. They have three children, but I have never been able to go there and they can't afford to come here. We're half a world apart. I don't know why God worked it out this way for me, but Gutsy is all the family I have had for a long, long time. If he has to be killed, I'll do it. It is up to me. Thank you, doctor."

The veterinarian started to protest again, but the old man had gathered his dog up in his arms and was at the door. I was in the process of opening it for him when he turned back.

"Gutsy and I really appreciate everything you have tried to do. We understand, truly we do."

The old man was gone, and the doctor was shaking his head as he reached for the next card in the wall rack.

We read about it the next day. It wasn't front-page news, by any means, but it did make most of the Boston dailies. The old man had gone home, stuffed paper under the door, sealed the windows, and placed his rocking chair in front of the stove. He turned the oven on, but he didn't light it. I am sure he was rocking slowly, perhaps humming reassuringly to Gutsy, as they both went to sleep. I cried. I think the veterinarian did, too. I know some of the other kennel kids did, and I resented those who didn't.

Little Lost Pup
ARTHUR GUITERMAN

He was lost!—not a shade of a doubt about that;
For he never barked at a slinking cat,
But stood in the square where the wind blew raw,
With a drooping ear and trembling paw
And a mournful look in his pleading eye
And a plaintive sniff at the passer-by
That begged as plain as a tongue could sue,
"O Mister, please may I follow you?"

A lorn wee waif of a tawny brown
Adrift in the roar of a heedless town—
Oh, the saddest of sights in a world of sin
Is a little lost pup with his tail tucked in!

Well, he won my heart (for I set great store
On my own Red Bute—who is here no more)
So I whistled clear, and he trotted up,
And who so glad as that small lost pup!
Now he shares my board, and he owns my bed,
And he fairly shouts when he hears my tread;
Then, if things go wrong, as they sometimes do,
And the world is cold and I'm feeling blue,
He asserts his right to assuage my woes
With a warm, red tongue and nice, cold nose
And a silky head on my arm or knee
And a paw as soft as a paw can be.

When we rove the woods for a league about
He's as full of pranks as a school let out;
For he romps and frisks like a three months' colt,
And he runs me down like a thunder-bolt,
Oh, the blithest of sights in the world so fair
Is a gay little pup with his tail in the air!

My Dog's Tail
ARTHUR WALLACE PEACH

What put the wiggle in a little dog's tail
  I'd like to know!
That gay little wiggle, that glad little waggle—
  How did it grow?

It starts in his mind and it runs out behind
  To the tip of his tail, and then
That glad little waggle, that gay little wiggle
  Begins all over again.

The day may be sunny or dark with rain,
  The wiggle is there just the same;
It needs just a whistle to set it a-wiggle
  Or the sound of his favorite name.

No doubt I shall never, in any way ever
  Find out how that wiggle got there,
But I'm very sure, while tails shall endure,
  That tail will wig-wag in the air!

Get Lost Buster, I'm in Charge Here

DR. BRUCE FOGLE

Once upon a time there was a Yorkshire Terrier named Fred. Fred was a tough nut. Like many of his breed he had, in spite of decades of inbreeding, maintained the Yorkie's basic terrier instincts to rape and pillage. He anointed every lampost, every hedge, every leaf, every blade of grass, every ant, proclaiming to all that cared to take a sniff, that this was Fred's territory. "Prepare to meet your doom all ye who enter here," he said with his urine.

Fred's territory marking was obsessive and he marked everywhere. It would have been more economical if he had been born with three legs, he kept one up in the air so long. Fred's ritual was to sniff, raise his left hind leg and deposit a drop of urine, thereby proclaiming the territory to be his, then turn from north to south or east to west, but in all cases a full 180 degrees, lift his right hind leg and mark again. Then, as my wife says, he "bopped"; he kicked up some earth with his hind legs (or regrettably some carpet or linoleum) leaving a physical mark to his terrain. Fred suffered from territory marking gone rampant and he was a nuisance whenever he was brought in for me to examine him, for aside from his urine marking proclivities he also protected his territory by barking—and any territory he was standing on, as far as Fred was concerned, was his.

I have a doorbell that clients have to ring and Fred's territorial imperative would begin there. As deft as a cat burglar and in full trot, he would leave his mark on the front door, the hall wall and the door to reception. He was so quick, even he probably didn't know how successful he was, and without breaking stride he would anoint the leg of a chair and the reception desk. Each time the doorbell rang he barked; he barked to protect his territory. Some dogs sing, others yodel, but barking is the commonest way a dog signals, "This is my place—get lost, buster."

Fred barked when the doorbell rang and he barked when he saw other visitors come into reception. I'm quite sure that dogs have no idea of their size, and little dogs certainly don't. Fred would challenge anything. All in all, between his barking and urine marking he had earned a distinct mark on his medical record card, a "P". Fred was a pest.

One day Fred was in reception while his owner waited for me to see him and a Pyrenean Mountain Dog came in. Fred danced at the end of his lead, barking, showing his teeth—smiling, as Yorkie owners describe it—and creating his usual obnoxious song and dance. His owner as always did nothing. The Pyrenean looked perplexed. He was probably familiar with fleas but this pipsqueak of an irritation looked, smelled and sounded like a dog, a male dog. And what was the midget trying to tell him? Was the little yapper actually saying, "Get lost, buster. This is *my* territory"? Did it really think that it could defend the reception room as his territory? The Pyrenean stiffened and looked straight at Fred, but Fred's display remained ferocious and he yapped and lunged at the bigger dog. So the Pyrenean walked over to Fred and drowned him. He peed all over him. Not just a symbolic drop but a torrent, enough for Fred to still look like a soaked rat five minutes later when I got around to seeing him and he had already been dried off. Fred shut up like a clam because he inherently understood territory games and he knew he was up against a real winner. The Pyrenean might have been pretty nonchalant about his business but he was a master at playing "Get lost, buster. I'm in charge here."

Dr. Fogle gives another example of territorial games:

The inside of a car is a nice neat territory for a dog to defend— enclosed, protected, den-like and almost always occupied by other members of his pack. It's a natural place to defend and even the

gentlest, most reliable pet can unexpectedly become a glazed sali-
vating monstrosity when a stranger approaches "his" car and he's
inside. John Steinbeck didn't know it when he wrote *Travels with
Charley,* but he eloquently and humorously described a classic
territory game. Steinbeck recounted driving with Charley into
Yellowstone National Park in this way:

> Less than a mile from the entrance I saw a bear beside
> the road and it ambled out as though to flag me down.
> Instantly, a change came over Charley. He shrieked with
> rage. His lips flared, showing wicked teeth that had some
> trouble with a dog biscuit. He screeched insults at the
> bear . . . I have never been so astonished in my life.
> To the best of my knowledge, Charley had never seen
> a bear, and in his whole history had shown great tolerance
> for every living thing. Besides all this, Charley is a coward,
> so deep seated a coward that he has developed a technique
> for concealing it. And yet he showed every evidence of
> wanting to get out and murder a bear that outweighed
> him a thousand to one.

Even a dog as civilized as Charley can't help but play "Get
lost, buster" when the circumstances direct him to do so.

Gone to the Dogs

WILLIAM HANKINS CHITWOOD

This country has literally gone to the dogs;
We've lost all our bearings and half of our cogs;
The butcher and baker, the valet and maid
Have turned to the canines for service and trade.

They come in all sizes, dimensions, and breeds
To answer the fashionable family's needs;
In fact, they are cherished so fondly today
The kidnaper frequently sneaks them away.

Why, even the fur coats that Nature provides
Are not deemed sufficient to cover their hides;
And so, emulating the town's gayest fops,
In doggish attire from Dogge Toggery Shoppes,
They step out in topcoats and zipper-bound sweaters,
And lounge in pajamas with monogrammed letters.

Our fears for their health have become more than fears;
They've turned into phobias within recent years;
We check them on scales till their weights are increased;
And dose them with vitamin extracts and yeast.

No wonder the millionaire packer of meats
Pays special attention to what the dog eats;
Or that the big merchant each season employs
More girls to sell owners dog-dainties and toys;

For, really the dog takes the LEAD in this land;
And man walks behind with a leash in his hand.

There's no doubt about it, we've sunk in the bogs
Of "civilization," and gone to the dogs,
Just look at the hospitals built for their care;
Sometimes there are THREE on the very same square.

The modern dog-doctor who knows his "profession,"
Treats owner and patient with equal discretion;
He thoroughly studies the owner's psychosis
Before he decides on the dog's diagnosis;
And, if he discovers a case of the "fleas,"
He calls it "phlebitis," and doubles his fees.

No wonder the druggist has turned more and more
To filling prescriptions for dogs in his store;
No wonder to them every grocery clerk kow-tows;
This country has gone to the "demnition bow-wows."

The Care and Training of a Dog
E. B. WHITE

There is a book out called *Dog Training Made Easy* and it was sent to me the other day by the publisher, who rightly guessed that it would catch my eye. I like to read books on dog training. Being the owner of dachshunds, to me a book on dog discipline becomes a volume of inspired humor. Every sentence is a riot.

Some day, if I ever get a chance, I shall write a book, or warning, on the character and temperament of the dachshund and why he can't be trained and shouldn't be. I would rather train a striped zebra to balance an Indian club than induce a dachshund to heed my slightest command.

For a number of years past I have been agreeably encumbered by a very large and dissolute dachshund named Fred. Of all the dogs whom I have served I've never known one who understood so much of what I say or held it in such deep contempt. When I address Fred I never have to raise either my voice or my hopes. He even disobeys me when I instruct him in something that he wants to do. And when I answer his peremptory scratch at the door and hold the door open for him to walk through, he stops in the middle and lights a cigarette, just to hold me up.

"Shopping for a puppy presents a number of problems," writes Mr. William Cary Duncan, author of *Dog Training Made Easy*. Well, shopping for a puppy has never presented many problems for me, as most of the puppies and dogs that have entered my life (and there have been scores of them) were not the result of a shopping trip but an act of God. The first puppy I owned, when I was about nine years old, was not shopped for—it was born to the collie bitch of the postman of my older sister, who sent it to me by express from Washington, D.C., in a little crate containing, in addition to the puppy, a bar of Peters' chocolate and a ripe frankfurter. And the puppy I own now was not shopped for but was won in a raffle. Between these two extremes there have been many puppies, mostly unshopped for. It is not so much that I acquired dogs as it is that dogs acquire me. Maybe they even shop for me, I don't know. If they do I assume they have many problems, because they certainly always arrive with plenty, which they then turn over to me.

The possession of a dog today is a different thing from the possession of a dog at the turn of the century, when one's dog was fed on mashed potato and brown gravy and lived in a doghouse with an arched portal. Today a dog is fed on scraped beef and Vitamin B$_1$ and lives in bed with you.

An awful lot of nonsense has been written about dogs by persons who don't know them very well, and the attempt to elevate the purebred to a position of national elegance has been, in the main, a success. Dogs used to mate with other dogs rather casually in my day, and the results were discouraging to the American Kennel Club but entirely satisfactory to small boys who liked puppies. In my suburban town, "respectable" people didn't keep she-dogs. One's washerwoman might keep a bitch, or one's lawn cutter, but not one's next-door neighbor.

The prejudice against females made a deep impression on me, and I grew up thinking that there was something indecent and unclean about she-things in general. The word bitch of course was never used in polite families. One day a little mutt followed me home from school, and after much talk I persuaded my parents to let me keep it—at least until the owner turned up or advertised for it. It dwelt among us only one night. Next morning my father took me aside and in a low voice said: "My son, I don't know whether you realize it, but that dog is a female. It'll have to go."

"But why does it have to?" I asked.

"They're a nuisance," he replied, embarrassed. "We'd have all the other dogs in the neighborhood around here all the time."

That sounded like an idyllic arrangement to me, but I could tell from my father's voice that the stray dog was doomed. We turned her out and she went off toward the more liberal section of town. This sort of incident must have been happening to thousands of American youngsters in those days, and we grew up to find that it had been permanently added to the record by Dorothy Parker in her short story "Mr. Durant."

On our block, in the days of my innocence, there were in addition to my collie, a pug dog, a dachshund named Brun, a fox terrier named Sunny who spent many years studying one croquet ball, a red setter, and a St. Bernard who carried his mistress's handbag, shuffling along in a stately fashion with the drool running out both sides of his jaws. I was scared of this St. Bernard because of his size, and never passed his house without dread. The dachshund was old, surly, and disagreeable, and was endlessly burying bones in the flower border of the DeVries's yard. I should very much doubt if any of those animals ever had its temperature taken rectally, ever was fed raw meat or tomato juice, ever was given distemper inoculations, or ever saw the whites of a veterinary's eyes. They were brought up on chicken bones and gravy and left-over cereal, and were all fine dogs. Most of them never saw the inside of their owner's houses—they knew their place.

The "problem" of caring for a dog has been unnecessarily complicated. Take the matter of housebreaking. In the suburbia of those lovely post-Victorian days of which I write the question of housebreaking a puppy was met with the simple bold courage characteristic of our forefathers. You simply kept the house away from the puppy. This was not only the simplest way, it was the only practical way, just as it is today. Our parents were in possession of a vital secret—a secret which has been all but lost to the world: the knowledge that a puppy will live and thrive without ever crossing the threshold of a dwelling house, at least till he's big enough so he doesn't wet the rug.

Although our fathers and mothers very sensibly never permitted a puppy to come into the house, they made up for this indignity by always calling the puppy "Sir." In those days a dog didn't expect anything very elaborate in the way of food or medical care, but he did expect to be addressed civilly.

Mr. Duncan discusses housebreaking at some length and assumes, as do all writers of dog books, that the owner of a puppy has little else to do except own the puppy. It is Mr. Duncan's theory that puppies have a sense of modesty and don't like to be stared at when they are doing something. When you are walking the dog, he says, you must "appear utterly uninterested" as you approach some favorite spot. This, as any city dweller knows, is a big order. Anybody who has ever tried to synchronize a puppy's bowels with a rigid office schedule knows that one's interest in the small phenomena of early morning sometimes reaches fever pitch. A dog owner may feign disinterest, but his masque will not suffice. Nothing is more comical than the look on the face of a person at the upper end of a dog leash, pretending not to know what is going on at the lower.

A really companionable and indispensable dog is an accident of nature. You can't get it by breeding for it, and you can't buy it with money. It just happens along. Out of the vast sea of assorted dogs that I have had dealings with, by far the noblest, the best, and the most important was the first, the one my sister sent me in a crate. He was an old-style collie, beautifully marked, with a blunt nose, and great natural gentleness and intelligence. When I got him he was what I badly needed. I think probably all these other dogs of mine have been just a groping toward that old dream. I've never dared get another collie for fear the comparison would be too uncomfortable. I can still see my first dog in all the moods and situations that memory has filed him away in, but I think of him oftenest as he used to be right after breakfast on the back porch, listlessly eating up a dish of petrified oatmeal rather than hurt my feelings. For six years he met me at the same place after school and convoyed me home—a service he thought up himself. A boy doesn't forget that sort of association. It is a monstrous trick of fate that now, settled in the country and with sheep to take care of, I am obliged to do my shepherding with the grotesque and sometimes underhanded assistance of two dachshunds and a wire-haired fox terrier.

Omar Meets a Toy

BURGES JOHNSON

Quite gentle is a St. Bernard,
    A Russian wolfhound is polite;
A Dane outside his own front yard
    Will almost never pick a fight.

But there's a midget lives near by—
    A cockroach must have been his sire—

With shivery legs and bulging eye
 And scolding yaps that never tire;

Who's always daring me to fight,
 Then running to his house and yelping.
If I should ever take a bite,
 There wouldn't be a second helping.

If things like that were on the ark
 I'll bet the beasts were all agog.
He has four legs, and he can bark—
 God made him—maybe he's a dog.

At the Dog Show
Ballad of a Languid Lady, or, My Dogs Hurt
PEG ROLAND

*This gay verse was inspired by that annual event of American
dogdom, The Westminster Kennel Club Show in Madison
Square Garden, New York City. (With apologies to C. Moore
and Santa Claus)*

T was the birthday of Lincoln and all thru the Garden
The din was terrific, an uproar we'll pardon.
Two days of dog days, and fast falling snow;
Such weather it was for a Westminster Show!
Of the dogs some were benched, some were penned in their
    crates,

From the judges above they waited their fates.*
Their owners and handlers rushed madly about
With high hopes of winning some ribbons, no doubt.

There were Scotties and Corgis and stately red Setters,
Retrievers and Mastiffs, all canine go-getters.
Hounds, Boxers, French Bulldogs, Salukis and Cockers,
They all had their boosters, and some had their knockers.
There were Yorkies and Poms and upstanding Schnauzers,
Beau Brummels and kids, and ladies in trousers.
Borzois and Dachsies, and all kinds of Terriers,
Wolfhounds and Afghans and even some Herriers.†

The exercise rings, one for dogs, one for bitches,
Were such fun to watch, we were often in stitches.
The basement was teeming with all kinds of ads
Pushing all kinds of dog food, and fashions, and fads.
Such brushing, such primping, such bright shining coats,
Such yipping, such yapping, such outlandish notes!
The rings above stairs, the parading and posing,
The impassioned pleas and the gentle bulldozing

To make poochie-pet step along—stop and go,
And eventually turn out to be Best in Show.
There were classes for youngsters; some smart little guys
Knew how to put many an old handler wise
To ways in the ring with recalcitrant curs††
That wanted to make with a scrap, rumbling gr-rs.§
All dog folk were there (I don't mean they're freaks,
But people in dogs whom we'd not seen in weeks).

The crowds filled the seats for row upon row,
Not a thing came to pass to louse up the show.
The judging of groups was a sight so inspiring

---

* Poetic License.
† More P.L. (I know how to spell it.)
†† For rhyming purposes only.
§ This one makes me a licensed poet.

That people watched hour upon hour without tiring.
Each group had its leader, each dog had its day,
But of the six victors, the best—who could say?
Diversions aplenty, 'twas right thrilling, too,
When those marvelous war dogs marched in for review.

They do sentry duty along with the boys,
Their sharp ears and eyes can detect every noise;
They locate the wounded and bring them relief,
They spy out the Nazis, who soon come to grief.
No foxhole escapes their keen vigilance
And villainous saboteurs don't have a chance.
Then a raffle and auction did much for the Cause,
The money rolled in with scarcely a pause.

The auctioneer's voice rang out clear as a bell
And some who bought War Bonds won puppies as well.
At long last came the time to pick Best in Show,
Which one for that spot? All were eager to know.
For Hound group the Foxhound, red Setter for Sporting,
The Yorkie and Poodle were in there cavorting.
The dignified Boxer was looking his best,
But—the little Welsh Terrier led all the rest!

To all who love dogs the show was a treat,
But somebody—give me a new pair of feet!

Shot

ALBERT PAYSON TERHUNE

Foremost among the Sunnybank dogs of my childhood and young boyhood was my father's oversized pointer, Shot. He is worth your notice. Naturally, in any modern dog show Shot would be "gated" most unmercifully.

He was of royally pure blood. But his head lacked the so-styled refinement of today's show pointer. His mighty chest and shoulders and hindquarters that carried him tirelessly for ten hours a day through the stiffest kinds of shooting country, and the harsh coat and thick skin which served as armor against briar and bramble and kept him unscathed through the thorniest copses—these were at laughable variance with the silken skin and dainty narrow-chested body lines of the show-type pointer of nowadays.

At "laughable" variance. But to me the laugh would not be on Shot. For, to me, he still is, in memory, the grandest pointer of my rather long experience.

My mother's health broke. My father took her and all of us to Europe, in the hope of curing her. (The cure was made. She lived more than forty healthy years longer.)

Sunnybank was rented during our two-year absence from America. Shot was sent to one of my uncles to be cared for until we should come back to him.

This uncle, Colonel G. P. Hawes, Sr., was an ideal sportsman. He understood dogs as it is given to few men to understand them. He and Shot had been good friends, since the pointer came to us as a just-weaned puppy. The dog could not have had a better home and a more congenial guardian.

Yet Colonel Hawes wrote my father that the usually gay dog had grown sullen and mopey and spiritless. Shot went through his duties in the hunting field as honestly as ever, but with no interest. He was grieving sorely for his absent master and for Sunnybank.

After our two-year exile we came back to America. One of my father's first moves was to go to my uncle's home and bring Shot to Sunnybank. He took me along on this errand. Its details are as clear in my memory as if they had occurred last month.

As soon as we were seated, Colonel Hawes sent a man to bring Shot into the house. The dog was kenneled some distance away and had not seen or scented our arrival. Into the living room plodded the pointer, at my uncle's summons.

He was thinner, much thinner, than I remembered him. His gait and his every line and motion were listless. He seemed wholly without spirit and devoid of any interest in life. My father had arranged the scene beforehand. He had told me what to do. I did it.

He and I sat motionless and without speaking. We were at the end of the room farthest from the door, and we were seated perhaps ten feet from each other.

Lifelessly, Shot came through the doorway. Just inside the threshold he halted. Up went his splendid head. His eyes sought out my father's mute and moveless figure. For a second or more the dog stood so.

Then he began to creep toward my father, hesitantly, one slow step at a time, crouching low and shuddering as with ague. Never did his dazed eyes leave my father's face. Inch by inch he continued that strangely crawling advance.

He did not so much as glance toward where I was sitting. His whole mind was focussed on the unmoving and unspeaking man in the chair ahead of him. So might a human move toward the ghost of a loved one; incredulous, hypnotized, awed. Then my father spoke the one word:

"Shot!"

The dog screamed as though he had been run over. He hurled himself on his long-lost master, sobbing and shrieking, insane with joy. Then the sedate pointer whirled around him in galloping circles, and ended the performance by dropping to my father's feet, laying his head athwart his shoe and chattering and sobbing.

I drew a shaky breath. At the sound Shot raised his head from its place of adoration.

He dashed over to me and accorded me a welcome which ordinarily would have seemed tumultuous, but which was almost indifferent, compared to the greeting he had accorded my father. Then, all at once, he was back to his master again, laying his head on the man's knee and still sobbing in that queerly human fashion.

(Yet not long ago I read a solemn scientific preachment to the effect that no dog could remember a lost master's face and scent for the space of eighteen months! Shot beat that record by half a year. And I believe he could have beaten it by a decade.)

To Sunnybank we came; Shot with us. The dog's sullen apathy was gone—gone for all time. He was jubilantly happy at his return to the home of his earliest memories. But for weeks he would not willingly let my father out of his sight. He seemed to fear he would lose his master again.

My father taught me to shoot. A few years after our return to America he and I went out quail-hunting with Shot. At the base of a steep hill there was a brambly meadow. The meadow was cut midway by a railroad track. As he neared the track, the dog came to a dead point. He was facing a clump of low bushes on the far side of the rails.

Statue-still, Shot stood, at point, waiting my father's signal to move forward toward the clump. Before that signal could be spoken, an express train came whizzing around the curve at the foot of the hill, and bore down toward us. Under its wheels and in its wake was a fog of dust and of flying hot cinders.

Shot stood, rocklike, on his point. The train roared past, not ten inches from his nose. The dog did not stir or falter, though he was peppered with burning cinders and choked by the whirlwind of dust and soot.

After the train had rattled its ill-smelling length out of the way, my father signaled Shot to move forward. The pointer took two stealthy steps ahead: steps that carried him to the center of the railroad track. From the clump just in front of him three quail whirred upward like a trio of fluffy little bombs. I suppose they had been too scared by the passage of the train to break cover until then.

Shot dropped to the ground, tense and waiting. My father brought down two of the birds in one of his customary brilliant left-and-right volleys.

Dog Wanted

MARGARET MACKPRANG MACKAY

I don't want a dog that is wee and effeminate,
Fluffy and peevish and coyly discriminate;
Yapping his wants in querulous tone,
Preferring a cake to a good honest bone.

I don't want a beast that is simply enormous,
Making me feel as obscure as a dormouse
Whenever he hurtles with jubilant paws
On my shoulders, and rips with his powerful claws
My sturdiest frocks; the kind of a mammal
That fits in a parlor as well as a camel,
That makes the floor shake under foot when he treads,
And bumps into tables and bounds over beds.

The sort of pet that I have in my mind
Is a dog of the portable, washable kind;
Not huge and unwieldy, not frilly and silly,
Not sleek and not fuzzy, not fawning, not chilly—
A merry, straightforward, affectionate creature
Who likes me as playmate, respects me as teacher,

And thumps with his tail when he sees me come near
As gladly as if I'd been gone for a year;
Whose eyes, when I praise him, grow warm with elation;
Whose tail droops in shame at my disapprobation;
No pedigreed plaything to win me a cup—
Just a portable, washable, lovable pup!

Lone Dog

IRENE RUTHERFORD MCLEOD

I'm a lean dog, a keen dog, a wild dog, and lone;
I'm a rough dog, a tough dog, hunting on my own;
I'm a bad dog, a mad dog, teasing silly sheep;
I love to sit and bay the moon, to keep fat souls from sleep.

I'll never be a lap dog, licking dirty feet,
A sleek dog, a meek dog, cringing for my meat,
Not for me the fireside, the well-filled plate,
But shut door, and sharp stone, and cuff and kick and hate.

Not for me the other dogs, running by my side,
Some have run a short while, but none of them would bide.
O mine is still the lone trail, the hard trail, the best,
Wide wind, and wild stars, and hunger of the quest.

The Dog Show:
Heaven Help Us

ROGER CARAS

The dog show. A fete as crazed as a block party in Iran, a celebration of the dog, of man, and of sporting ambition, a sporting event as genteel on the surface as the U.S. Open but as heavy underneath as a hockey game. All of that and more. The first recorded event of this kind took place in 1859 in Newcastle-on-Tyne. There were six judges pinching and prodding sixty pointers and setters. The next year, 1860, there was a show in Birmingham as well. The idea stuck and has never come unstuck. The fact that prickly people can make it a little sticky at times has done nothing to dull the sport's luster. It was and is a fine idea even if it does appear at times to have been invented by a sardonic prankster.

If animals bring out both the best and the worst in people, and it is my premise that they do, the dog show magnifies all that several score times. The better get better and the worst get incredibly worse. A dog show is a cross between an office picnic, a bloodless bullfight, root-canal work, a Miss America pageant, and a tax audit by an IRS person who is jealous of you, as they all are. You get most of your flat tires of the year going to dog shows, take most of your wrong turns and get your most iridescent sunburns and best soakings, all the while wondering not only what everyone else around you is doing, but what you are doing yourself, perhaps even *to* yourself.

. . . . As long as people respect dogs and have concern for their own accomplishments, the history of their own taste and sense of style, and as long as human beings appreciate beauty, the purebred dog as a piece of genetic art will be fostered. The best way to keep it all going, to select the best, to eliminate that which does not represent intent in style and beauty, is to engage in a sport called dog shows. As for the elitists who put stickers like CAUTION: SHOW DOGS on the back of their cars and rigs, may they get what they deserve. After all, a sticker like that seems to be boasting of money (which show dogs by no means represent today as they once did), and anyone who wants to boast of being loaded, with the crime rate what it is today, is probably asking for broken windows and missing possessions. One hopes their dogs will not suffer. Dogs, show or otherwise, never use bumper stickers except to urinate on . . .

Our Dumb Friends

RALPH WOTHERSPOON

My home is a haven for one who enjoys
The clamor of children and ear-splitting noise
From a number of dogs who are always about,
And who want to come in and, once in, to go out.
Whenever I settle to read by the fire,
Some dog will develop an urge to retire,
And I'm constantly opening and shutting the door
For a dog to depart or, as mentioned before,
For a dog to arrive who, politely admitted,
Will make a bee-line for the chair I've just quitted,
Our friends may be dumb, but my house is a riot,
Where I cannot sit still and can never be quiet.

Verse for a Certain Dog

DOROTHY PARKER

Such glorious faith as fills your limpid eyes,
 Dear little friend of mine, I never knew.
All-innocent are you, and yet all-wise.
 (For Heaven's sake, stop worrying that shoe!)
You look about, and all you see is fair;
 This mighty globe was made for you alone.
Of all the thunderous ages, you're the heir.
 (Get off the pillow with that dirty bone!)

A skeptic world you fare with steady gaze;
 High in young pride you hold your noble head;
Gayly you meet the rush of roaring days.
 (Must you eat puppy biscuit on the bed?)
Lancelike your courage, gleaming swift and strong,
 Yours the white rapture of a winged soul,
Yours is a spirit like a May-day song.
 (God help you, if you break the goldfish bowl!)

"Whatever is, is good"—your gracious creed.
 You wear your joy of living like a crown.
Love lights your simplest act, your every deed.
 (Drop it, I tell you—put that kitten down!)
You are God's kindliest gift of all—a friend.
 Your shining loyalty unflecked by doubt,
You ask but leave to follow to the end.
 (Couldn't you wait until I took you out?)

Rx: One Loving Animal
BETTY WHITE

Let me tell you about Billy. Eight years old, Billy underwent six leg operations. His leg failed to heal properly, and making matters worse, both Billy and his mother seemed to be giving up hope.

"I am going to prescribe a medicine that will surprise you," his doctor announced to the mother one day. "I want you to go out and get a puppy. It will do you both good."

A little mongrel with big funny ears, a moist black nose, huge paws, and brown eyes (guaranteed to pass the audition) was found for Billy, and her presence was felt immediately. For the first time in weeks, Billy laughed. He named his puppy Brownie Gal, and stroked her and combed her and cuddled her in his arms.

The little dog allowed both Billy and his mother to divert their attention from his injured leg, and at long last, the limb began to heal. As the doctor later reported, "The dog was helping the whole family get out of themselves." And Brownie Gal was actually knitting them closer together.

One morning a few weeks later, Billy struggled to his feet and asked for his crutches. "I've got to learn to do this," he explained, "because Brownie Gal needs me to walk her."

The Hairy Dog
HERBERT ASQUITH

My dog's so furry I've not seen
His face for years and years;
His eyes are buried out of sight,
I only guess his ears.

When people ask me for his breed,
I do not know or care;
He has the beauty of them all
Hidden beneath his hair.

I Think I Know
No Finer Things Than Dogs
HALLIE CARRINGTON BRENT

Though prejudice perhaps my mind befogs,
I think I know no finer things than dogs:
The young ones, they of gay and bounding heart,
Who lure us in their games to take a part,

Who with mock tragedy their antics cloak
And, from their wild eyes' tail, admit the joke;
The old ones, with their wistful, fading eyes,
They who desire no further paradise
Than the warm comfort of our smile and hand,
Who tune their moods to ours and understand
Each word and gesture; they who lie and wait
To welcome us—with no rebuke if late.
Sublime the love they bear; but ask to live
Close to our feet, unrecompensed to give;
Beside which many men seem very logs—
I think I know no finer things than dogs.

The Thin Red Leash
JAMES THURBER

It takes courage for a tall thin man to lead a tiny Scotch terrier pup on a smart red leash in our neighborhood, that region bounded roughly (and how!) by Hudson and West Streets, where the Village takes off its Windsor tie and dons its stevedore corduroys. Here men are guys and all dogs are part bull. Here "cute" apartments stand quivering like pioneers on the prairie edge.

The first day that I sallied forth with Black Watch III bounding tinily at the street end of the thin red leash, a cement finisher, one of the crowd that finds an esoteric pleasure in standing on the bleak corner of Hudson and Horatio Streets, sat down on the sidewalk and guffawed. There were hoots and whistles.

It was apparent that the staunch and plucky Scotch terrier breed was, to these uninitiated bulldog-lovers, the same as Pekingese. But Black Watch must have his airing. So I continued to brave such witticisms as "Hey, fella, where's the rest of it?" and—this from a huge steamfitter—"What d'y say me an' you an' the dog go somewheres and have tea?"

Once a dockworker demanded, in a tone indicating he would not take Black Watch III for an answer, "What's that thing's name?"

My courage failed me. "Mike," I said, giving the leash a red-blooded jerk and cursing the Scotty. The whole affair was a challenge to my gumption. I had been scared to call my dog by its right name.

The gang was on hand in full force the next evening. One of them snapped enormous calloused fingers at Black Watch and he bounded away, leash and all, from my grasp.

"Black Watch!" I shouted—if you could call it shouting.

"What did y' call that dog, fella?" demanded a man who, I think, blows through truck exhaust whistles to test them.

"Black Watch," said I.

"What's that mean?" he asked menacingly.

"It was a Scottish regiment wiped out at Ypres or somewhere," I said, pronouncing it "Eeprr."

"Wiped out where?" he snarled.

"Wiped out at Wipers," I said.

"That's better," he said.

I again realized that I had shown the white feather. That night I took a solemn, if not fervent, oath to tell the next heavy-footed lout that flayed my dog to go to hell. The following evening the gang was more numerous than ever. A gigantic chap lunged forward at us. He had the build of a smokestack-wrecker.

"Psst!" he hissed. Black Watch held his ground.

"They're scrappers, these dogs," I protested amiably.

"What d' they scrap—cockroaches?" asked another man, amid general laughter. I realized that now was the time to die. After all, there are certain slurs that you can't take about your dog— gang or no gang. Just then a monstrous man, evidently a former Hudson Duster who lifts locomotives from track to track when the turntables are out of order, lounged out of a doorway.

"Whadda we got here?" he growled.

"Park Avenoo pooch," sneered one gas-house gangster. The train-lifter eyed Black Watch, who was wagging his tail in a most friendly manner.

"Scotty, ain't it?" asked the train-lifter, producing a sack of scrap tobacco.

"Yeah," I said, as easily as I could.

"Damn fine dogs, Scotties," said the train-lifter. "You gotta good 'un there, when it puts on some age, scout. Hellcats in a fight, too, *I* mean. Seen one take the tonsils out of a Airedale one day."

"Yeah?" asked the smokestack-wrecker.

"Yeah," said the train-lifter.

"Yeah," said I.

Several huge hands went down to pat a delighted shaggy head. There were no more catcalls or hoots. Black Watch III had been acquitted of Pomeranianism. We're quite good friends now, Black Watch and the gang and I. They call him Blackie. I am grateful to a kind Fate that had given the train-lifter the chance, between carrying locomotives, to see a Scotty in action.

My Dog
MARCHETTE CHUTE

His nose is short and scrubby;
   His ears hang rather low;
And he always brings the stick back,
   No matter how far you throw.

He gets spanked rather often
   For things he shouldn't do,

Like lying-on-beds, and barking,
  And eating up shoes when they're new.

He always wants to be going
  Where he isn't supposed to go.
He tracks up the house when it's snowing—
  Oh, puppy, I love you so!

Quality

MARTY HALE

My little dog lies curled asleep
Beside my cozy fire—
Close as the spark-screen will permit,
His nose against the wire;
He is a rather homely mutt,
His body gaunt and slim—
He counts on me but doesn't know
How much I count on him.
He doesn't know how very much
His friendship means to me—
Or how his tiny little frame
Can give me security;
He doesn't know I'm farther off
From things of worth than he—
Or that he's very much the things
God meant that I should be.
I search for things of quality

As down life's path I jog—
I miss them in my human friends,
But find them in my dog.

Blemie's Will

EUGENE O'NEILL

I Silverdene Emblem O'Neill (familiarly known as Blemie), because the burden of my years and infirmities is heavy upon me,
and I realise the end of my life is near, do hereby bury my last
will and testament in the mind of my master. He will not know
it is there until after I am dead. Then, remembering me in his
loneliness, he will suddenly know of this testament, and I ask
him to inscribe it as a memorial to me.

I have little in the way of material things to leave. Dogs are
wiser than men. They do not waste their days hoarding property.
They do not ruin their sleep worrying about how to keep the
objects they have now. There is nothing of value I have to bequeath
except my love and my faith. These I leave to all those who have
loved me, to my master and mistress, who I know will mourn
me most . . . Perhaps it is vain of me to boast when I am so
near death, which returns all beasts and vanities to dust, but I
have always been an extremely lovable dog.

I ask my master and mistress to remember me always, but not
to grieve for me too long. In my life I have tried to be a comfort
to them in time of sorrow, and a reason for added joy in their
happiness. It is painful for me to think that even in death I should
cause them pain. Let them remember that while no dog has had
a happier life (and this I owe to their love and care for me), now

that I have grown blind and deaf and lame, and even my sense
of smell fails me so that a rabbit could be right under my nose
and I might not know, my pride is sunk to a sick, bewildered
humiliation. I feel life is taunting me with having over-lingered
my welcome. It is time I said goodbye, before I become too sick
a burden on myself and those who love me. It will be a sorrow
to leave them, but not a sorrow to die. Dogs do not fear death
as men do. We accept it as part of life, not as something alien
and terrible which destroys life. What may come after death, who
knows? I would like to believe with those of my fellow Dalmatians
who are devout Mohammedans, that there is a Paradise where
one is always young and full-bladdered; where all the day one
dallies and dillies with an amorous multitude of houris, beautifully
spotted . . .

I am afraid this is too much for even such a dog as I am to
expect. But peace, at least, is certain. Peace and long rest for
weary old heart and head and limbs, and eternal sleep in the
earth I loved so well. Perhaps, after all, this is best. One last
request I earnestly make. I have heard my mistress say, "When
Blemie dies we must never have another dog. I love him so much
I could never love another one." Now I would ask her, for love
of me, to have another. It would be a poor tribute to my memory
never to have a dog again. What I would like is that, having
once had me in the family, now she cannot live without a dog
. . . To him I bequeath my collar and leash and my overcoat
and raincoat, made to order in 1929 at Hermes in Paris. He can
never wear them with the distinction I did, walking around the
Place Vendôme, or later along Park Avenue, all eyes fixed on
me in admiration, but again I am sure he will do his utmost not
to appear a mere gauche provincial dog . . . One last word of
farewell, dear master and mistress. Whenever you visit my grave,
say to yourselves with regret but also happiness in your hearts at
the remembrance of my long happy life with you: "Here lies one
who loved us and whom we loved." No matter how deep my
sleep I shall hear you, and not all the power of death can keep
my spirit from wagging a grateful tail.

Dog in Chair

MARGARET MACKPRANG MACKAY

Aha! I've caught you there again!
I'm really very angry—when
I've told you fifty times or more,
A puppy's place is on the floor,
And not upon an easy chair.
You've made the cover thick with hair,
And left the print of dirty paws,
And pulled the threads with scratching claws.
I simply will not have you in it.

The moments pass, and by and by,
Out of the corner of my eye,
I see you softly, gently creeping
Across the rug, and nimbly leaping
Upon the chair's inviting seat.
What shall I do? Again repeat
My scolding? No, I'll let it rest;
The ostrich method is the best.
Although we both know where your place is,
At least we're saving both our faces!

Welcome Home
LOUELLA C. POOLE

I saw him coming up the street,
So spent and weary that his feet
  Seemed like two heavy weights of lead;
Ah, he had known so hard a day,
Small wonder that he looked that way,
  And slouched along with drooping head!

Then, suddenly, with frantic shout,
A little yellow dog rushed out
  A yard, to greet the tired man;
He licked his hands, he kissed his face,
Then dashed ahead in eager race,
  Then back again he gaily ran!

The tired worker laughed aloud,
Straightened his shoulders; through the crowd
  Pressed on; his feet seemed to take wings
So fast he walked as he went up
The street toward home, the yellow pup
  All joyous leaps and caperings.

O little dog so fond and true,
Much good in life you surely do
  When you can make a man so spent
Forget fatigue—make him so glad
He acts like any madcap lad,
  And laughs aloud with merriment!

Living With People
DR. BRUCE FOGLE

Patrick Payence, a colleague who practices in Paris, has analysed the names that his clients give to their pets and again it is interesting that the majority give their pets human names like Victor and Sophie. Twenty-five per cent of his clients still give their pets animal names like Minou. Animal names such as Rover, Spot and Lassie are on the wane in England simply because as life gets more hectic pets are playing a more involved role in families. That role is difficult to explain but in part involves our need to escape, or at least to have breaks from the increasing pressures and tensions of a crowded and competitive urban life. And as our world has become more hectic we have looked upon our pets, bred them and named them, to satisfy our anthropomorphic needs. Sometimes however this goes too far.

In the 1970s I frequently used to see a well-known politician, an aggressive law and order man, and his pet gun dog. Whenever he talked to his dog he lapsed into babytalk, and on the odd occasion when he had to leave his dog with me for the day his regression into this childlike behaviour was actually embarrassing.

Regression is important in all of us because the child in us contributes to our charm and helps our creativity, but with this man, this outwardly tough guy, I couldn't help but feel that deep down inside he needed someone to hug but was afraid of showing his feelings to another person, so his dog, his non-judgmental gun dog, was the recipient of his feelings. This is pretty easy to do because most people see a smaller emotional distance between themselves and their pets than between themselves and other people.

As I have said, the child in us is in many ways our most valuable part and contributes pleasure to our family life. Breeding dogs to perpetuate childlike qualities, spontaneity, intuitiveness and a care-free nature, adds to the great pleasure that they give us. It also helps us because through our pets we can, at least for a little while, return to a gentler and more natural way of life.

When Honey was younger I used to take her each lunchtime for her daily exercise in Hyde Park. Because she was so obedient, she walked unfettered, without a lead, for the short distance to the park. She stopped at each intersection, waited for the signal, then ran full tilt to the next intersection and waited for me. At the crosswalk at Bayswater Road, her last obstacle, she would stamp her feet with excitement and give me a constant, yearning, pleading, expressive look until I told her to proceed. Then she would dash into the park and tumble and roll in a state of near oblivion.

Honey was quite convinced that those daily excursions were only for her benefit and she wasn't altogether wrong. But they were for me too. There are times when being an adult is just no fun. Polite talk. Use of the grey matter. Responsibility. All these things can become oppressive sometimes. The benefits of civilization don't help either. Traffic noise. Telephones. Bustle. Pet owners. Those daily walks with Honey, though, always brought a feeling of contentment. Sure, it wasn't the same as a paddle at dawn on a mirror-smooth mist-covered lake, but it was still an escape even if I was still in the heart of London, and what made it so was that dog's sniffing and investigating and rolling on worm mounds, meeting with circumspection other dogs and dashing headlong for the Serpentine to pretend she was a submarine. Robert Bench-ley said, "There is no doubt that every healthy, normal boy should own a dog at some time in his life, preferably between the ages of forty-five and fifty." The humorist was a clever psychologist. The symbolic childlike behaviour of my dog is what gave me so much pleasure.

Friendship
MARTY HALE

My dreams were crumbled, and my house
Of cards came tumbling down—
And all my bright air castles
Had fallen to the ground;
I swore there was no loyalty,
Friendship a myth, and so
I'd never trust in them again,
My lovely dreams must go—
And then I heard the pat of paws,
The click of little toes,
And in my hand there snuggled close
A little cold, wet nose!

A Toast
JUNE PROVINE

I raise . . . my glass to all good dogs.
To no particular breed, no special strain
Of certified prize winners—just to plain
Unpedigreed Good Dogs. . . .
I drink to wagging tails and honest eyes,
To courage and unguessed-at loyalties,
Whose values never will be known or sung.

The Animal With A Conscience
KONRAD LORENZ

Author-naturalist Konrad Lorenz recalls an experience with a male English bulldog that belonged to a neighboring family:
. . . Bonzo, as the dog was called, was savage with strangers but docile toward friends of the family, and he not only knew me well but would greet me politely and even enthusiastically whenever our paths happened to cross. I was once invited to tea at Schloss Altenberg, the home of Bonzo and his mistress. I drew up on my motorcycle in front of the castle, which occupies a lonely position in the forest. I had dismounted and, with my back to the door, was bending down to adjust the stand of the machine, when Bonzo shot out and, quite understandably failing to recognize my overall-clad backside, seized my leg in his teeth and hung on in true bulldog style. I yelled out his name in agonized tones, whereupon he fell as though shot by a gun and groveled before me on the ground. As there had obviously been a misunderstanding and as in any case my thick outfit had prevented serious injury—a few bruises on the shinbone do not matter to a motorcyclist—I spoke encouragingly to Bonzo, caressed him and was ready to forget it. But not so the bulldog. The whole afternoon he followed me round and at tea he leaned against my leg. Every time I looked at him he sat up very straight, fixed on me his protruding bulldog eyes and pleaded forgiveness by frantically offering his paw. Some days later when we met in the road, he did not greet me in his usual boisterous fashion, but in the same attitude of humility, giving me his paw, which I shook heartily.

Understanding
MARGARET E. BRUNER

Sometimes it seems as if a dog can sense
One's thoughts more quickly than a human can;
They know the moments that are dark and tense—
When worries have upset life's general plan.
And I have seen them gazing into space
At such a time, as if they almost knew
That any gesture would be out of place
Unless one asked for it. How very few
Of all the wise and learned of earth possess
This strange, uncanny power to understand
Man's deepest moods of utter loneliness,
When naught but silence meets the heart's demand.

Heritage
STANTON A. COBLENTZ

Place not your faith in blood. We are controlled
By currents deeper than the flesh. Behold
The fierce, blood-trailing wolf-pack's progeny:
Man's friend and chum, the dog against your knee!

A Dog's Lot

JAMES THURBER

If Man has benefited immeasurably by his association with the dog, what, you may ask, has the dog got out of it? His scroll has, of course, been heavily charged with punishments: he has known the muzzle, the leash, and the tether; he has suffered the indignities of the show bench, the tin can on the tail, the ribbon in the hair; his love life with the other sex of his species has been regulated by the frigid hand of authority, his digestion ruined by the macaroons and marshmallows of doting women. The list of his woes could be continued indefinitely. But he has also had his fun, for he has been privileged to live with and study at close range the only creature with reason, the most unreasonable of creatures.

The dog has got more fun out of Man than Man has got out of the dog, for the clearly demonstrable reason that Man is the more laughable of the two animals. The dog has long been bemused by the singular activities and the curious practices of men, cocking his head inquiringly to one side, intently watching and listening to the strangest goings-on in the world. He has seen men sing together and fight one another in the same evening. He has watched them go to bed when it is time to get up, and get up when it is time to go to bed. He has observed them destroying the soil in vast areas, and nurturing it in small patches. He has stood by while men built strong and solid houses for rest and quiet, and then filled them with lights and bells and machinery. His sensitive nose, which can detect what's cooking in the next township, has caught at one and the same time the bewildering smells of the hospital and the munitions' factory. He has seen men raise up great cities to heaven and then blow them to hell.

The effect upon the dog of his life with Man is discernible in his eyes, which frequently are capable of a greater range of expression than Man's. The eyes of the sensitive French poodle, for example, can shine with such an unalloyed glee and darken with so profound a gravity as to disconcert the masters of the earth, who have lost the key to so many of the simpler magics. Man has practiced for such a long time to mask his feelings and to regiment his emotions that some basic quality of naturalness has gone out of both his gaiety and his solemnity.

The dog is aware of this, I think. You can see it in his eyes sometimes when he lies and looks at you with a long, rueful gaze. He knows that the bare foot of Man has been too long away from the living earth, that he has been too busy with the construction of engines, which are, of all the things on earth, the farthest removed from the shape and intention of nature. I once owned a wise old poodle who used to try to acquaint me with the real facts of living. It was too late, though. I would hastily turn on the radio or run out and take a ride in the car.

The Dog

OGDEN NASH

The truth I do not stretch or shove
When I state the dog is full of love.
I've also proved, by actual test,
A wet dog is the lovingest.

Obituary

E. B. WHITE

Daisy ("Black Watch Debatable") died December 22, 1931, when she was hit by a Yellow Cab in University Place. At the moment of her death she was smelling the front of a florist's shop. It was a wet day, and the cab skidded up over the curb—just the sort of excitement that would have amused her, had she been at a safer distance. She is survived by her mother, Jeannie; a brother, Abner; her father, whom she never knew; and two sisters, whom she never liked. She was three years old.

Daisy was born at 65 West Eleventh Street in a clothes closet at two o'clock of a December morning in 1928. She came, as did her sisters and brothers, as an unqualified surprise to her mother, who had for several days previously looked with a low-grade suspicion on the box of bedding that had been set out for the delivery, and who had gone into the clothes closet merely because she had felt funny and wanted a dark, awkward place to feel funny in. Daisy was the smallest of the litter of seven, and the oddest.

Her life was full of incident but not of accomplishment. Persons who knew her only slightly regarded her as an opinionated little bitch, and said so; but she had a small circle of friends who saw through her, cost what it did. At Speyer Hospital, where she used to go when she was indisposed, she was known as "Whitey," because, the man told me, she was black. All her life she was subject to moods, and her feeling about horses laid her sanity open to question. Once she slipped her leash and chased a horse for three blocks through heavy traffic, in the barking belief that she was an effective agent against horses. Drivers of teams, seeing her only in the moments of her delirium, invariably leaned far out of their seats and gave tongue, mocking her; and thus made themselves even more ridiculous, for the moment, than Daisy.

She had a stoical nature, and spent the latter part of her life an invalid, owing to an injury to her right hind leg. Like many invalids, she developed a rather objectionable cheerfulness, as though to deny that she had cause for rancor. She also developed, without instruction or encouragement, a curious habit of holding people firmly by the ankle without actually biting them—a habit that gave her an immense personal advantage and won her many enemies. As far as I know, she never even broke the thread of a sock, so delicate was her grasp (like a retriever's), but her point of view was questionable, and her attitude was beyond explaining to the person whose ankle was at stake. For my own amusement, I often tried to diagnose this quirkish temper, and I think I understand it: she suffered from a chronic perplexity, and it relieved her to take hold of something.

She was arrested once, by Patrolman Porko. She enjoyed practically everything in life except motoring, an exigency to which she submitted silently, without joy, and without nausea. She never took pains to discover, conclusively, the things that might have diminished her curiosity and spoiled her taste. She died sniffing life, and enjoying it.

An Introduction to Dogs

OGDEN NASH

The dog is man's best friend.
He has a tail on one end.
Up in front he has teeth.
And four legs underneath.

Dogs like to bark.
They like it best after dark.

They not only frighten prowlers away
But also hold the sandman at bay.

A dog that is indoors
To be let out implores.
You let him out and what then?
He wants back in again.

Dogs display reluctance and wrath
If you try to give them a bath.
They bury bones in hideaways
And half the time they trot sideways.

Dogs in the country have fun.
They run and run and run.
But in the city this species
Is dragged around on leashes.

Dogs are upright as a steeple
And much more loyal than people.
Well people may be reprehensibler
But that's probably because they are sensibler.

Hero

ALBERT PAYSON TERHUNE

They named him "Hero." This was when he was only two months old and his loud barks defied the world. He was such a fearless little fluff of gold-brown fur that the name seemed to fit every active inch of him. A year later, however, the name "Hero" fitted him as a double-width woolen blanket might fit a ladybug.

The Marriotts had been very proud of the rabbit-sized collie baby. But the Marriotts were very ashamed of the rabbit-hearted collie giant that Hero had grown into.

True, he was beautiful. But his deep-set dark eyes had not the "look of eagles" a collie's eyes should have. In them was gentleness, but not a hint of spirit.

"I don't mind his being gentle," grumbled Rance Marriott. "Gentleness is the grandest thing in the world. But if it hasn't spirit and strength behind it, it isn't gentleness at all."

"But Hero's so obedient and friendly," protested Hilda Marriott. "He's never the least bother, and—"

"And never the least joy, either," added her husband.

"I hate a quarrelsome dog!" put in Hilda.

"So do I," agreed Rance. "But one wants his dog to be something more than a sheep. Whenever I'm walking with him and we pass the Brendas', that husky police dog of Sam Brendas' comes charging out. He tackled Hero in earnest, the first time. Nowadays he does it for a joke. He sails into Hero and knocks him over and rolls him in the gutter and nips him, until I interfere. Does Hero take his own part? He does not! He just sprawls there meekly and lets himself be rough-housed. Then when the police dog has been driven off, Hero gets up and trots along with me not at all ashamed that he's been licked. It's the same when a cur half his size tackles him. Hero just curls up and lets himself be thrashed."

Out on the veranda bounded the big bronze collie, his expression almost excited—for Hero. Up to Rance and then to Hilda he capered, barking and galloping back to the front door, and returning to repeat the performance.

"What's happened?" wondered Rance. "He looks almost alive. Is it a new game he's invented or—"

"He wants us to go somewhere with him," said Hilda. "See how he runs from one to the other of us and back to the hallway. Come along."

As they started toward the hall, Hero gamboled delightedly ahead to the top of the cellar stairs. There he waited only long enough to make certain his owners were close behind him. Then down the stairs he pattered.

"Come along!" begged Hilda, as Rance hesitated. "Let's see what he's trying to show us."

"A man-eating mouse, probably," suggested Rance. "But, no, that can't be. For he'd never have the sublime courage to approach a mouse, of his own accord."

The dog came running up the steps, whined eagerly, and trotted down again. This time the Marriotts followed. At the foot of the stairs Rance turned on the electric switch, flooding the shadowy place with light.

Hero was standing proudly above a pile of soft rags in a far corner. On the rag couch lay the Marriotts' gray Persian cat, Fathma, blinking lazily up at them. Cuddled against her furry underbody squirmed four tiny and varicolored newly born kittens.

Fathma was strangely easygoing, for a Persian. She and Hero had been brought up together. They had always been on comfortable terms, their mutual mildness serving to avert quarrels.

Now, Hero was excited at discovering Fathma's children. As soon as Rance and Hilda bent over the rag bed to look at the kittens, the collie rushed up the back cellar stairs to the kitchen. Presently he reappeared, coaxing the cook down to view the newcomers.

Fathma lay there and purred, blinking sleepily. Now and then she licked one or another of her babies with a rough pink tongue.

That night Hero did not sleep on his rug outside Hilda Marriott's door, where he had slept ever since he was a puppy. Instead, he stretched his mighty bulk on the concrete floor of the cellar, as close as might be to Fathma and her babies.

"He's found his true role in life, at last," sneered Rance. "As a collie he is a grand kitten-nurse."

Hilda did not join in her husband's mirth. To her there was something pathetic in the huge dog's absorbed interest in the family of newly born baby cats and in his air of protection over them. True, it was undoglike, and especially was it uncollie-like. But it did not seem funny to her.

That was the beginning. Every day, and practically all day, and every night and all night, Hero lay or sat or stood guard over the litter of Persians. Gravely he would survey the fast-growing kittens, sometimes touching them gingerly with his forepaw or sniffing at them.

He was in misery when a load of coal rattled noisily down the chute, and he interposed his own bulk between it and the corner where the kittens were.

One day he and Fathma had their first quarrel. Playfully Hero rolled one of the kittens over with his nose. He was unintentionally rough. The kitten squalled in protest. Fathma flew to the rescue, side-swiping Hero across the nostrils with sharp claws.

The dog fled, howling, until he reached the top of the cellar stairs. There he stood, in comic dismay, slapping alternately at his scratched and bleeding nose, and peering fearfully down at the scene of his ill-treatment.

Step by step, at long intervals, he descended to the cellar and crept trembling along the floor until once more he was near the nest. Fear of further punishment made him shake as with a chill. But the craving to return to his duty as guard overcame his dread.

To his relief, Fathma made no attempt to renew the strife. Nor did Hero make further playful advances toward the kittens. He contented himself sniffing at them now and then, and lying quietly with head between his forepaws, watching.

Rance often took guests down to the cellar to see the kittens' canine nurse. With all a collie's odd sensitiveness, Hero seemed to realize he had become an object of ridicule. He winced and cringed when laughter greeted the spectacle of a great bronze dog brooding over a nestful of kittens. But he did not desert his post.

The babies grew larger and stronger. No longer did they content themselves with huddling in the nest. Now, with sprawling feet and unwieldy little fat bodies, they set forth on exploring expeditions along the cellar floor. A pretty sight it was to watch the fluffy mites crawling about the delighted big dog, while their sleepy mother looked placidly on.

One of them in particular, a snow-white kitten with china-blue eyes, picked Hero as her own chum. She would climb over his paws or cuddle against his chest or play with his plumed tail.

Pleased and proud was Hero of this distinction. He would lick the kitten all over. He would lie uncomplaining as her sharp claws dug playfully into his sensitive tail. The other kittens did not show any great interest in him. Thus, from the start, he and the white kitten were exclusive play fellows and pals.

Fathma was a good mother, as Persian mothers go. But she was a family pet, and her place had been upstairs with the humans of the household. When her kittens were able to get along without her for an hour or two at a time, she would leave them with Hero and would run daintily upstairs to seek out Hilda or Rance or the servants.

When the kittens were graduated from the cellar to the woodshed and were allowed to play daily on the lawn in the spring sunshine, Hero and the white kitten had gorgeous romps together. Their friendship was pretty to watch. Even Rance Marriott grinned with grudging approval of their play.

"Of course, it was just like the poor fool to pick out the kitten we're selling first," Rance said. "I suppose Hero will mope around and look more like a sick calf than ever, when she's gone. I'm sorry for him. For he's found the one creature on earth that doesn't either bully him or despise him."

"I don't bully him," denied Hilda, "and I don't despise him. And I wish you hadn't promised Sam Brendas that particular kitten. You know how fond Hero is of her, and—"

"And I had promised Sam his choice of the four," interrupted Rance. "I'm sorry to have to disappoint the noble Hero. Sam is sending for the kitten tomorrow afternoon. Will you have her brushed up a bit beforehand, please? And stick Hero in a closet or somewhere."

Mid-afternoon, next day, Hilda Marriott came out on the lawn, where Hero snoozed with the white kitten cuddled up asleep between his paws. Picking up the furry wisp in her arms, Hilda whistled to the dog. Happily he trotted indoors after her and his kitten pal. There, to his pained surprise, he was lured into an upper room and the door was shut behind him.

He scratched plaintively at the door, but nobody came to let him out. In a little while he heard voices downstairs—Hilda's voice and another woman's.

Readily the dog recognized this second voice. It belonged to a guest who came often to the Marriotts'. She lived in the house where that snarling police dog lived—the dog that mishandled Hero so unmercifully.

Failing to scratch his way through the door, the collie amused himself by trotting to the window and gazing down into the street. Then Hero's interest sharpened. Mrs. Sam Brendas had left the Marriott house and was walking down the street. In her arms she was carrying something.

As she turned the corner, Hero saw what the "something" was. It was his chum, his pal, his idol—the tiny white Persian kitten!

Something went queer in Hero's gentle brain.

The spirit of his brave collie ancestors suddenly seemed to assert itself. These collies had guarded with their lives their masters' belongings. They had known stanch loyalty to their friends.

Back to the door Hero ran, tearing at its panels with claws and teeth. It stood firm.

To the window he dashed. The room was on the second floor, just above the side veranda. But, for all Hero cared it might have been on the thirtieth story of a skyscraper. It offered the only means of escape—and he took his chance.

With a great diving leap he flung himself at the glass pane. Through the brittle barrier he crashed with all the driving force of his seventy pounds. He struck against the steep veranda roof, rolling and sliding down it to the edge, then bouncing out into space again. His falling body struck the center of a thick, high lilac clump, just beyond the porch. The branches broke his fall, so that he landed on the grass unhurt.

By the time he hit the lawn he was on his feet and in flying motion. Across the yard he sped and down the street galloping with his glass-cut body close to earth and with hackles bristling. He knew well where Mrs. Sam Brendas lived, and where she was carrying his kitten friend. Not an inch did he swerve from his route.

Men were beginning to stroll up the street on their way home from business. They gave wide berth to the bleeding, savagely onrushing collie.

A dog or two came running out from dooryards. Hero whizzed past them, unheeding. Some of them started to chase him. But no dog, save a racing greyhound, can hope to catch up with a collie that is running at full speed.

Hero came in sight of his goal in time to see Mrs. Brendas

open her own front door and disappear in the hallway. She was carrying the sacred white kitten. The kitten was scared because a giant police dog had sprung up from the mat and had come toward her. "Down!" Mrs. Brendas ordered the dog sharply and took the kitten indoors.

As the door shut behind her, Hero came dashing up the walk. The police dog's temper had been ruffled by the scent of the strange kitten and by his owner's curt rebuff. The collie had invaded the sanctity of the front yard and was rushing toward the sacredly guarded veranda. The insolence of his act called for a drastic and dramatic punishment. As Hero leaped up the veranda steps, the police dog dashed savagely after him.

Perfect love casteth out fear.

In all his despised young life Hero had never found anything worth losing his temper over. He had seen no need to fight. He had had no desire in his gentle heart to harm anyone or anything.

When he had been attacked and bullied by other dogs, their enmity had puzzled and pained him. He had seen no reason for fighting back. It had been easier to submit gently to their onslaughts and then to get himself out of their way as soon as he could.

But today he had something to fight for. His fluffy little white playmate had just been carried into that house, and an ugly giant dog was trying to bar him from following and rescuing her. The dog, and every other obstacle, must be gotten rid of before Hero could continue his search for the kitten.

Instead of the meekly crouching collie, the police dog found his charge met by a devil swathed in shimmering bronze fur. Grappling, roaring, slashing, rending, the two combatants rolled down the steps together. As their falling bodies hit the flagstones of the path below, they flashed apart and to their feet, flinging themselves at each other's throats.

This was the sight which confronted Rance Marriott and Sam Brendas, as together they rounded the corner of the street. This was the sight which made Mrs. Brendas drop the white kitten and run to the front door in consternation.

The police dog was a renowned battler and a veteran of many

bloody frays. But a fighting collie is not like any other fighter in all dogdom.

Hero was everywhere in general and nowhere in particular. Now he was stabbing with lightning speed under the rearing enemy's forelegs, and slashing the other's fawn-colored underbody. Now he was slipping eel-like from what threatened to be a death grip and was raking the police dog's tawny shoulder. So do wolves fight.

Once and again the larger dog tried to down Hero by sheer weight and ferocity. Once and again the collie eluded the charge, and countered with deep bite or slash. Twice Hero was knocked off his flying feet. But a collie down is almost never a collie beaten.

He fell with his feet bunched under him; and by the time he hit ground he was either springing to one side, slashing as he leaped, or rolling compactly out of range of the frightful jaws.

It was a beautiful exhibition of science against bull strength. Roaring and foaming, the police dog drove once more for the throat. The collie ducked under the great lunging head and dug his teeth with wrenching force into one of the fawn-hued forelegs of his foe. Thus does the wolf seek to cripple an antagonist by breaking his legs.

With a screech, the police dog released his grip on Hero's neck, and tried to seek safety in retreat.

Hero stood for a moment, panting and eyeing the victim. Then he seemed to remember his mission at that house. Up the steps he rushed, pushing past the panic-stricken Mrs. Brendas and into the hallway.

In another second he emerged. Between his bloody jaws he carried tenderly a fluff of white fur. He had found and rescued his little chum after overcoming the dragon which guarded the door. Now he was bearing her home where she belonged.

Past the men he cantered, deaf to Marriott's call. Two minutes later he laid the kitten gently at Hilda Marriott's feet. Then, apparently, he remembered that his master had called him and that he had not obeyed. Licking the kitten's tousled fur once in rough good-fellowship, Hero left her there and cantered out of the house.

Meantime both men had found their tongues.

"I get the whole idea!" Rance declared. "Hero loves that kitten as he doesn't love anything else. He came here after it. Your dog stopped him, but he couldn't stop him for long. Then Hero went in and got what he came for. You can guy me, if you like, you people. Hero fought for her and he won her, fair. You can have your cash back or you can have any two of the three other kittens instead. But you can't have the white one. Neither can anyone else. She belongs to Hero. Is that understood?"

Sam Brendas looked up from his task of tending his police dog's hurts.

"All right," he agreed. "We can settle the terms later on. Now give me a hand in carrying Hindenburg indoors, while Mary phones for the vet."

As Marriott came out of the Brendas' house three minutes later on his way home, a figure arose stiffly from the police dog's favorite porch mat and came in gay good-fellowship to greet him.

Rance stared down at his collie. Not at the cuts and other hurts that decorated his splendid body, but at the deep-set dark eyes upraised to his. Those eyes flashed with a queer light that changed the whole expression of Hero's classic face.

"The true collie look!" babbled Rance foolishly, as he caught the hurt head lovingly between his two hands. " 'The look of eagles!' Hero—"

His voice thickened in his throat. But Hero understood. Wagging his plumed tail, he led the way out of the gate and toward home. As they turned the corner into their own street, a neighbor's dog swaggered blusteringly out. This was a mongrel dog that delighted to chase Hero under the Marriott veranda every time he could catch him in the roadway.

In something less than half a minute, now, the mongrel aggressor was *ki-yi*-ing, in astonished flight, to the safety of his own kennel.

"Hero!" rebuked Marriott fondly, as he called his frisking collie back to him. "You'd be a grand walking companion if it wasn't that you have one bad fault—you're too quarrelsome. Try to get over the habit of going around with a chip on your shoulder, you—you glorious pal of mine!"

Lost Dog
FRANCES RODMAN

He lifts his hopeful eyes at each new tread,
Dark wells of brown with half his heart in each;
He will not bark, because he is well-bred,
Only one voice can heal the sorry breach.
He scans the faces that he does not know,
One paw uplifted, ear cocked for a sound
Outside his sight. Only he must not go
Away from here; by honor he is bound.
Now he has heard a whistle down the street;
He trembles in a sort of ecstasy,
Dances upon his eager, padding feet,
Straining himself to hear, to feel, to see,
And rushes at a call to meet the one
Who of his tiny universe is sun.

My Dog and I
ISLA PASCHAL RICHARDSON

You sit beside my chair. Your gaze
Unwavering and deep shines through
A shaggy fringe of hair. I shrink—
Unworthy of your estimate

Of me, your steadfast loyalty.
What are the thoughts behind those clear
And searching eyes? My enemies
And friends both see me as I am—
A mortal full of frailties.
And you, whose love would follow me
Into the deepest pit of woe,
I wonder if you do not see beyond
The erring human self of me,
Beholding all the good I would
Embody, all the heights I seek.
Yet unattained? Do you look through
The failures and mistakes and see
Me as the man I want to be?

At My Side

ALBERT PAYSON TERHUNE

Of all my countless ignorances of dog nature, the densest is
his yearning to be near his master or mistress.

I don't know why my collies will leave their dozing in front of
the living-room hearth for the privilege of following me out into
a torrent of winter rain. They hate rain.

I don't know why all folk's dogs risk gladly a scolding or a whipping
by breaking out of a room or a kennel into which they have been
shut, and galloping down the street or over the fields to catch
up with the master who purposely has left them behind.

Today (for another and non-thrilling instance) I am writing at
my hammock desk, a hundred yards or more from the house.

Seven dogs are with me. It is a cool, brilliant afternoon; just the weather for a romp. The lawns and the woods and the lake all offer allurement to my collies.

What are the seven doing? Each and every one of them is lounging on the ground, close to the hammock.

Even crippled and ancient Sandy (Sunnybank Sandstorm) has left the veranda mat where he was so comfortable. To him all movement nowadays is a source of more or less keen discomfort. Yet he limped painfully down the six steps from the veranda to the driveway, and came slowly over to me, as soon as he found I was here; stretching himself at my feet, on bumpy ground much less comfortable than his porch bed. And here for the past two hours he has been drowsing with the others.

Why? *I* don't know. There must be some mysterious lure in the presence of their human gods which gives dogs that silly yearning to stay at their sides, rather than to do more amusing and interesting things.

Beyond the Grave
MARGARET E. BRUNER

How often have we known a dog to be
   More loyal than the race of humankind . . .
Although it seems a dog can somehow see
   The very inmost caverns of the mind.

And yet he never looks upon a friend
   With scorn, even though the world that friend despise;

And when death claims his master—brings an end
   To comradeship—he grieves . . . his sorrowing eyes

Seem questioning, and yet to understand
   That this is something that must come to all,
But human folk can turn to tasks at hand
   To break the tension of its gloomy thrall.

It may be that the selfsame power that gave
   The dog his faithful, understanding heart
Will grant him life again beyond the grave,
   To meet with friends—where death can play no part.

To a Dog, Grown Blind

MAZIE V. CARUTHERS

Safe tethered by his master's loving hand
Against all passing dangers, nowadays
He who once chased the squirrels, fetched a ball,
Raced with the leaves, within a garden stays—
Sometimes he naps then restless, roams about
Seeking new bearings in this strange dark maze.

He turns his patient muzzle toward the sun,
But, patient, does not whine against his fate;
At each day's close there comes a step for which
An old dog listening eagerly can wait—
Then cautiously he stumbles down the path
To meet his master at the garden gate.

Their Absolute All
ROGER CARAS

Dogs have always subsisted on handouts. We give them the love we can spare, the time we can spare, the room we can spare. Even the best of the balanced dog foods, although meticulously compounded, consist of what we can spare from the slaughterhouse and what we can grow on the land we can spare. In return, dogs have given us their absolute all. We are the center of their universe, we are the focus of their love and faith and trust. They serve us in return for scraps. It is without a doubt the best deal man has ever made.

To My Dog
JOHN GALSWORTHY

My dear! When I leave you
I always drop a bit of me—
A holy glove or sainted shoe—
Your wistful corse I leave it to,
For all your soul has followed me—

How could I have the stony heart
So to abandon you!

My dear! When you leave me
You drop no glove, no sainted shoe;
And yet you know what humans be—
Mere blocks of dull monstrosity!
My spirit cannot follow you
When you're away, with all its heart
As yours can follow me.

My dear! Since we must leave
(One sorry day) I you, you me;
I'll learn your wistful way to grieve;
Then through the ages we'll retrieve
Each other's scent and company;
And longing shall not pull my heart—
As now you pull my sleeve!

The Joy of a Dog
EDGAR A. GUEST

Ma says no, it's too much care
An' it will scatter germs an' hair,
An' it's a nuisance through and through,
An' barks when you don't want it to;
An' carries dirt from off the street,
An' tracks the carpets with its feet.

But it's a sign he's growin' up
When he is longin' for a pup.

Most every night he comes to me
An' climbs a-straddle of my knee
An' starts to fondle me an' pet,
Then asks me if I've found one yet.
An' ma says: "Now don't tell him yes;
You know they make an awful mess,"
An' starts their faults to catalogue.
But every boy should have a dog.

An' some night when he comes to me,
Deep in my pocket there will be
The pup he's hungry to possess
Or else I sadly miss my guess.

For I remember all the joy
A dog meant to a little boy
Who loved it in the long ago,
The joy that's now his right to know.

Memorial

JAMES THURBER

She came all the way from Illinois by train in a big wooden
crate many years ago, a frightened black poodle, not yet a year
old. She felt terrible in body and worse in mind. These contraptions
that men put on wheels, in contravention of that law of nature

which holds that the feet must come in contact with the ground in traveling, dismayed her. She was never able to ride a thousand yards in an automobile without getting sick at her stomach, but she was always apologetic about this frailty, never, as she might well have been, reproachful.

She tried patiently at all times to understand Man's way of life: the rolling of his wheels, the raising of his voice, the ringing of his bells; his way of searching out with lights the dark protecting corners of the night; his habit of building his beds inside walls, high above the nurturing earth. She refused, with all courtesy, to accept his silly notion that it is better to bear puppies in a place made of machined wood and clean blue cloth than in the dark and warm dirt beneath the oak flooring of the barn.

The poodle was hand in glove with natural phenomena. She raised two litters of puppies, taking them in her stride, the way she took the lightning and the snow. One of these litters, which arrived ahead of schedule, was discovered under the barn floor by a little girl of two. The child gaily displayed on her right forearm the almost invisible and entirely painless marks of teeth which had gently induced her to put down the live black toys she had found and wanted to play with.

The poodle had no vices that I can think of, unless you could count her incurable appetite for the tender tips of the young asparagus in the garden and for the black raspberries when they ripened on the bushes in the orchard. Sometimes, as punishment for her depredations, she walked into bees' nests or got her long shaggy ears tangled in fence wire. She never snarled about the penalties of existence or whimpered about the trials and grotesqueries of life with Man.

She accepted gracefully the indignities of the clipping machine which, in her maiden days, periodically made a clown of her for the dog shows, in accordance with the stupid and unimaginative notion that this most sensitive and dignified of animals is at heart a buffoon. The poodle, which can look as husky as a Briard when left shaggy, is an outdoor dog and can hold its own in the field with the best of the retrievers, including the Labrador.

The poodle won a great many ribbons in her bench days, but she would have traded all her medals for a dish of asparagus.

She knew it was show time when the red rubber bib was tied around her neck. That meant a ride in a car to bedlam.

Like the great Gammeyer of Tarkington's *Gentle Julia*, the poodle I knew seemed sometimes about to bridge the mysterious and conceivably narrow gap that separates instinct from reason. She could take part in your gaiety and your sorrow; she trembled to your uncertainties and lifted her head at your assurances. There were times when she seemed to come close to a pitying comprehension of the whole troubled scene and what lies behind it. If poodles, who walk so easily upon their hind legs, ever do learn the little tricks of speech and reason, I should not be surprised if they made a better job of it than Man, who would seem to be surely but not slowly slipping back to all fours.

The poodle kept her sight, her hearing, and her figure up to her quiet and dignified end. She knew that the Hand was upon her and she accepted it with a grave and unapprehensive resignation. This, her dark intelligent eyes seemed to be trying to tell me, is simply the closing of full circle, this is the flower that grows out of Beginning; this—not to make it too hard for you, friend—is as natural as eating the raspberries and raising the puppies and riding into the rain.

A Friend

ESTHER BIRDSALL DARLING

At the battle of Chateau-Thierry, [during World War I] a young American army officer and his men arrived at an abandoned farm house that had been used as a German headquarters. Everything had been left in utter confusion, and on the threshold of the door they found a magnificent German Shepherd dog, dead; his side torn by shrapnel. He had dragged himself three hundred yards in a welter of blood, to try to deliver a message from a pocket of Germans asking for reinforcements.

The Americans were so touched by his gallantry that, tired and hungry as they were, they decided to give him a military funeral at once. One young sergeant, from Maryland, a lover of dogs, made a cross of two pieces of wood and on it wrote "Only a dog but as loyal a subject as the Kaiser had." The officer in command took the indelible pencil from him and added the last four lines of the following poem:

> Sometimes when life has gone wrong with you,
> And the world seems a dreary place,
> Has your dog ever silently crept to your feet,
> His yearning eyes turned to your face?
> Has he made you feel that he understands,
> And all that he asks of you
> Is to share your lot, be it good or ill,
> With a chance to be loyal and true?
> Are you branded a failure? He does not know.
> A sinner? He does not care.
> You're "master" to him—that's all that counts.
> A word, and his day is fair.
> Your birth and your station are nothing to him;
> A palace and hut are the same,
> And his love is yours, in honor and peace,
> As it's yours through disaster and shame.
> Though others forget you and pass you by,
> He is ever your faithful friend,
> Ready to give you the best that is his—
> Unselfishly unto the end!

Sleeping Habits of the Neurotic Dog

STEPHEN BAKER

Some dog owners refuse to share their beds with pets. For these people, the following step-by-step procedure of how to get a dog off the bed may be helpful.

First, get the dog within reach of your hands. Start out with gentle persuasion. If this fails to have any effect, and it always does, begin use of legs and body. Undulating movements of torso may roll the dog toward you so you can grab him. Push forcefully now, using your hands. If he bites, tear off part of the sheet for bandage.

If your dog is under the blanket (and most smarter breeds prefer this location) do not grope for him blindly. The wisest course is to lift up the blanket gradually. This is best achieved by getting out of bed. Do not yank the blanket off quickly since sudden movements will annoy the dog and he will fight for what he thinks belongs to him.

It is entirely possible that the dog will remain asleep even after you have taken the cover off. Try the pillow method. If the pillow bursts, do not despair, you can always buy a new one. Then jump up and down on the mattress for a few minutes.

At this point some dogs (those known as "watch dogs") will slowly open one or both eyes, although they will probably not be willing to leave the bed. Your next move is to rock the bed. Lift one end of the bed, then drop it firmly on the floor. Pull off the mattress. Turn the whole bed over.

If all these efforts come to nothing, let him know that you mean business. Impress on the dog that you're the sort of fellow who

sticks with his convictions; you will *not* share your bed with him.
Get another blanket from the linen closet and go to sleep on the
living room sofa.

The Bulldog Speaks
A. C. GATE

I agree that I'm no beauty
But I've got a Sense of Duty.
I've a face that stops 'em cold
But I've got a Heart of Gold.
Though I'm Dracula-appearing
I've a temperament that's cheering.

Is mere handsomeness your goal,
Or the Quality of Soul?
Bulldog-lovers are above
Surface thinking in their love.
Is the goal for which you strike
Character Gibraltar-like?

Are you one to underrate
Loyalty, that Sterling Trait?
There would be a big demand for
Bulls if folks knew what we stand for.
Never mind mere beauty's lures,
Think of stanchness that endures.
Think of Yale that brought us fame—
Or are you a Harvard dame?

The Best Medicine
ROGER CARAS

Clearly, I am not the one to ask for an objective evaluation of the role of dogs in the life of man. But I have been studying the subject all my life, just as I have been living it, and although I cannot give the mythical dispassionate view of this ancient love affair, I can remember some of its joys and share a little esoterica. Did you know, for example, that you will probably live longer, at least statistically, if you own dogs, one or more? Did you know that your blood pressure will be far easier to hold at a healthy level if you are a pet keeper than if you are not? Scientific studies bear this out. Pets are extremely good for your whole cardiovascular system, not to mention your psyche. You are less likely to commit suicide, less likely to take offense at what people do to you, if you have the leveling influence of a dog at some key points in the day to make the bad things go away. The dog does not judge you, and not being judged in the midst of our heavily judging and judged existence is like a life preserver in the middle of the sea. It virtually spells salvation for a great many people, especially young people being pulled at from all sides by peers, parents, teachers, and a blossoming libido.

The Yellow Dog

EDGAR A. GUEST

It was a little yellow dog,
  A wistful thing to see,
A homely, skinny, battered pup,
  As dirty as could be;
His ribs were showing through his hide,
  His coat was thick with mud,
And yet the way he wagged his tail
  Completely captured Bud.

He had been kicked from door to door
  And stoned upon his way,
"Begone!" was all he'd ever heard,
  'Twas all that folks would say;
And yet this miserable cur,
  Forever doomed to roam,
Struck up a comradeship with Bud,
  Who proudly brought him home.

I've nev'r seen so poor a dog
  In all my stretch of years,
The burrs were thick upon his tail
  And thick upon his ears;
He'd had to fight his way through life
  And carried many a scar,
But still Bud brought him home and cried:
  "Say, can I keep him, Ma?"

Dog Abandoned
INEZ CLARK THORSON

A dog, abandoned in the hills,
Still looking where the highways wind;
Still keeping faith with those who left
Him and then broken trust behind.

No smoke-wreaths curl above the house—
No children romping in the yard;
Through loneliness and storm and sun
He waits, though all the doors are barred.

He cannot know the Judas coin
With which his loyalty is paid,
Who waits with hunger-hollowed eyes
For those by whom he was betrayed.

In a Shop Window
MARGARET E. SANGSTER

He was such a little puppy, in a window of a shop,
And his wistful eyes looked at me, and they begged me please
    to stop
And buy him—for a window's awful lonely, and folk pass
And they make strange, ugly faces and rap sharply on the glass!

He was such a cunning beggar, and his paws were soft and wide,
And he had a way of standing with his head held on one side,
And his mouth just slightly open, and he always seemed to cry:
"Take me from this horrid window, 'cause I'm ready, most to
    die!"

He got tangled in my heart-strings, made me want to break away
From the lease I signed so gladly—was it only yesterday?
Said that dogs were not admitted . . . He was not a dog, not
    yet!
Only just a tiny puppy—and his nose was black and wet.

Did you ever speak unkindly of the friend you hold most dear?
Did you ever call out crossly, so that bystanders could hear?
Did you ever pull a curtain to shut out the smiling day?
That's how I felt—but more so—as I turned and walked away!

The Lonely Dog

MARGARET E. BRUNER

He often came and stood outside my door
And gazed at me with puzzled, wondering eyes,
Like those of humankind by grief made wise—
Who feel that life has little left in store.
And yet, he never looked unkempt and poor
As if he deemed a meaty bone a prize;
Instead, it seemed he wore a human guise
As though the heart of man he would explore.

Then one night on the street he followed me
Persistently, until I turned and said
Sharp, angry words, which made him quickly flee—
His spirit wounded and uncomforted,
And now at last I think I comprehend:
He only craved an understanding friend.

A Prayer for Dogs
GOLDIE CAPERS SMITH

Good Master, bless each dog that no one owns,
That has no flower bed to bury bones,
No loving hand to scratch his ears and ruff,
No gate to guard, and never quite enough
To eat. Ye saints, guard well each cringing pup
That slink with tail turned down instead of up.

Good Master, pity pampered city dogs
That sleep indoors all day like snoring logs,
That never feel the sun nor watch the rain—
Except behind a curtained window-pane;
That grow to wheeze and cough from too much fat,
And never in their lives have chased a cat.

All other dogs, beloved and gay and free,
Are blest enough—they need not trouble Thee.

What Makes the Dog Neurotic
STEPHEN BAKER

Today's dog lives under more pressure than ever before in history. His schedule is demanding; chores confront him every minute of the day. The heavy strain put on the modern dog causes many to crack up.

Here is a typical schedule of the average dog of today.

7:30– 7:55	Thinks about getting up.
7:55– 8:00	Jumps off bed; shakes thoroughly. Ambles to kitchen where there seems to be some activity.
8:00– 8:15	Participates at the breakfast table.
8:15–10:00	Walks back to the bedroom. Sleeps.
10:00–11:30	Accompanies mistress of the house as she shops. At the supermarket, lifts a bag of peanuts from the lowest shelf. Chase. Eats on the run. Loses mistress and has to walk home.
11:30–12:00	Before-meal nap in bedroom.
12:00–12:45	Adjourns to living room sofa. Continuation of nap.
12:45– 1:30	Chased off sofa. Back to bedroom in search of privacy. Nap.
1:30– 2:30	Ejected from bedroom. Removed from sofa. Walks down to basement. Nap.
2:30– 2:50	Greets children returning from school. Jumps up and down, wags tail, licks faces, etc., to make good impression.
2:50– 2:51	Eats meal of dog food.
2:51– 3:15	Participates at meal with children and their mother.
3:15– 3:30	After-meal nap.
3:30– 4:00	Calls on neighbor, a dachshund named Mozart. Joins rest of gang in search of female companionship. Visits Julie, a Pekingese, but finds she is locked up in the house for some reason. Too bad.
4:00– 4:15	Fights with the boys.

4:15– 4:16	Takes short cut across the Taylor's garden.
4:16– 4:30	Pursued by Mrs. Taylor. Boys disperse.
4:30– 4:35	Leaps into stream to lose Mrs. Taylor. She can't swim.
4:35– 4:45	Enters living room. Lifted up by back of neck and put out the back door with orders to dry off.
4:45– 5:30	Nap in garage.
5:30– 6:30	Helps mistress of house get dinner ready.
6:30– 7:30	Participates at family dinner.
7:30– 7:55	Watches television, an adult Western. Naps through second half of program.
7:55– 8:00	Awakened by shooting on television. Badman falls off horse. He's dead. Continues nap.
8:00– 8:01	Walks to bedroom.
8:01	Retires.

confession of a glutton

don marquis

after i ate my dinner then i ate
part of a shoe
i found some archies by a bathroom pipe
and ate them too

i ate some glue
i ate a bone that had got nice and ripe
six weeks buried in the ground
i ate a little mousie that i found
i ate some sawdust from the cellar floor
it tasted sweet
i ate some outcast meat
and some roach paste by the pantry door
and then the missis had some folks to tea
nice folks who petted me
and so i ate
cakes from a plate
i ate some polish that they use
for boots and shoes
and then i went back to the missis swell tea party
i guess i must have eat too hearty
of something maybe cake
for then came the earthquake
you should have seen the missis face
and when the boss came in she said
no wonder that dog hangs his head
he knows hes in disgrace
i am a well intentioned little pup
but sometimes things come up
to get a little dog in bad
and now i feel so very very sad
but the boss said never mind old scout
time wears disgraces out

What's Better Than a Dog?
MICHAEL W. FOX

A dog is a faithful companion for the lonely or aged; a watchdog for the frightened people in our crime-ridden cities and suburbs; a trusting and always willing playmate, sometimes even a reliable baby-sitter; a "second person" without whom a blind man, a shepherd, a night watchman or an infantry patrol in the jungle would be helpless and ineffectual. Above all, a dog is a dog, and knowing something about him, about his ways, his needs and how he develops, we can learn more about the world around us and about ourselves and enrich our own lives and the knowledge of our children beyond measure.

A Dog
EDGAR A. GUEST

Tis pity not to have a dog,
  For at the long day's end
The man or boy will know the joy
  Of welcome from a friend.
And whether he be rich or poor
  Or much or little bring,

The dog will mark his step and bark
  As if he were a king.

Though gossips whisper now and then
  Of faults they plainly see,
And some may sneer, from year to year
  My dog stays true to me.
He's glad to follow where I go,
  And though I win or fail
His love for me he'll let me see
  By wagging of his tail.

Now if I were to list the friends
  Of mine in smiles and tears
Who through and through are staunch and true
  And constant down the years,
In spite of all my many faults
  Which critics catalog
Deserving blame, I'd have to name
  My ever-faithful dog.

'Tis pity not to have a dog,
  Whatever be his breed,
For dogs possess a faithfulness
  Which humans sadly need.
And whether skies be blue or gray,
  Good luck or ill attend
Man's toil by day, a dog will stay
  His ever-constant friend.

Mongrel Type Dog

HENRY MORGAN
GEORGE BOOTH

This is your patchwork kind of friend. He is made of spare parts. Like many of us, his folks didn't think too much about Planned Parenthood. Like most of us, his blood lines are blurred.

And, like most of us, he is the most kind of dog there is.

Well, genealogy isn't everything. When you stop to think of it very few people can trace their ancestry back to Beowulf. And a lot of us are lucky if we can get past Calvin Coolidge.

When somebody says to somebody else, "Just what kind of dog is that?" and the somebody else replies, "Oh, he's half and half," that isn't the half of it. The reason for this is that each of the halves is probably nothing to write the American Kennel Club about.

A purebred dog may be too much of a good thing. You take your average, pedigreed, certified, vouched for and sworn to and testified animal and you'll find you've got a snob on your hands. Mister Elegance won't lower himself to, say, chase a rabbit. Why should he? He's accustomed to three-minute eggs, moist pâté de foie gras—but not too moist—and things like brandy and after-dinner cigars. Rabbits, he thinks, are for the underadvantaged.

One of the first things we noticed about the average mongrel is that there isn't any. Still, they do have one thing in common. Even though they come in one million shapes and sizes and colors, they are all wonderful because each and every one of them fits a kid.

The Dog Who Paid Cash
WILL ROGERS

While I didn't have anything else to do, I got to watching an old spotted dog. He was just an ordinary dog, but when I looked at him close, he was alert and friendly with everyone. Got to inquiring around and found out he'd been bumped off a freight train and seemed to have no owner. He made himself at home and started right in business. When a crowd of cowboys would go into a saloon, he would follow 'em in and begin entertaining. He could do all kinds of tricks—turn somersaults, lay down and roll over, sit up on his hind feet, and such like.

He would always rush to the door and shake hands with all the newcomers. The boys would lay a coin on his nose, and he'd toss it high in the air and catch it in his mouth and pretend to swallow it. But you could bet your life he didn't swallow it— he stuck it in one side of his lip and when he got a lip full of money, he'd dash out the back door and disappear for a few minutes. What he had really done was hide his money. As soon as he worked one saloon, he would pull out and go to an- other place.

I got to thinking while watching this old dog, how much smarter he is than me. Here I am out of a job five hundred miles from home and setting around and can't find a thing to do, and this old dog hops off a train and starts right in making money, hand over fist.

Me and some boys around town tried to locate his hidden treasure but this old dog was too slick for us. He never fooled away no time on three or four of us boys that was looking for work. He seemed to know we was broke, but he was very friendly. As he was passing along by me, he'd wag his tail and kinda wink. I musta looked hungry and forlorn. I think he wanted to buy me a meal.

When times was dull and he got hungry, he would mysteriously disappear. Pretty soon he'd show up at a butcher shop with a dime in his mouth and lay it on the counter and the butcher would give him a piece of steak or a bone. He always paid for what he got in the line of grub. Pretty soon he seemed to get tired of the town, and one morning he was gone. A railroad man told us later that he seen the same dog in Trinidad, Colorado.

The Outlaw
ROBERT W. SERVICE

There is a very filthy fellow who collects cigarette stubs on Boul' Mich', and who is always followed by a starved yellow cur. The other day I came across them in a little side street. The man was stretched on the pavement brutishly drunk and dead to the world. The dog, lying by his side, seemed to look at me with sad, imploring eyes. Though all the world despised that man, I thought, this poor brute loves him and will be faithful unto death. From this incident I wrote the verse that follows:

> A wild and woeful race he ran
> Of lust and sin by land and sea;
> Until, abhorred of God and man,
> They swung him from the gallows-tree.
> And then he climbed the Starry Stair,
> And dumb and naked and alone,
> With head unbowed and brazen glare,
> He stood before the Judgment Throne.

The Keeper of the records spoke:
"This man, O Lord, has mocked Thy Name.
The weak have wept beneath his yoke,
The strong have fled before his flame.
The blood of babes is on his sword;
His life is evil to the brim:
Look down, decree his doom, O Lord!
Lo: there is none will speak for him."

The golden trumpets blew a blast
That echoed in the crypts of Hell,
For there was Judgment to be passed,
And lips were hushed and silence fell.
The man was mute; he made no stir,
Erect before the Judgment Seat . . .
When all at once a mongrel cur
Crept out and cowered and licked his feet.

It licked his feet with whining cry.
Come Heav'n, come Hell, what did it care?
It leapt, it tried to catch his eye;
Its master, yea, its God was there.
Then, as a thrill of wonder sped
Through throngs of shining seraphim,
The Judge of All looked down and said:
"Lo! here is ONE who pleads for him.

"And who shall love of these the least,
And who by word or look or deed
Shall pity show to bird or beast,
By Me shall have a friend in need.
Aye, though his sin be black as night,
And though he stand 'mid men alone,
He shall be softened by My sight,
And find a pleader by My Throne."

"So let this man to glory win;
From life to life salvation glean;

By pain and sacrifice and sin,
Until he stand before Me—*clean*
For he who lovest the least of these
(And here I say and here repeat)
Shall win himself an angel's pleas
For Mercy at My Judgment Seat."

Fashions in Dogs

E. B. WHITE

An Airedale, erect beside the chauffeur of a Rolls-Royce,
Often gives you the impression he's there from choice.

In town, the Great Dane
Is kept by the insane.

Today the boxer
Is fashionable and snappy;
But I never saw a boxer
Who looked thoroughly happy.

The Scotty's a stoic,
He's gay and he's mad;
His pace is a snail trot,
His harness is plaid.
I once had a bitch,
Semi-invalid, crazy:

There ne'er was a Scotch girl
Quite like Daisy.

Pekes
Are biological freaks.
They have no snout
And their eyes come out.
Ladies choose'm
To clutch to their bosom.
A Pekinese would gladly fight a wolf or a cougar
But is usually owned by a Mrs. Applegate Kruegar.

Cockers are perfect for Elizabeth Barrett Browning,
Or to carry home a package from the A. & P. without clowning.

The wire-haired fox
Is hard on socks
With or without clocks.
The smooth-haired variety
Has practically vanished from nice society,
And it certainly does irk us
That you never see one except when you go to the circus.

The dachshund's affectionate,
He wants to wed with you:
Lie down to sleep,
And he's in bed with you.
Sit in a chair,
He's there.
Depart,
You break his heart.

My Christmas will be a whole lot wetter and merrier
If somebody sends me a six-weeks-old Boston terrier.

Sealyhams have square sterns and cute faces
Like toy dogs you see at Macy's.

But the Sealyham, while droll in appearance,
Has no clearance.

Chows come in black, and chows come in red;
They could come in bright green, I wouldn't turn my head.
The roof of their mouth is supposed to be blue,
Which is one of those things that might easily be true.

To us it has never seemed exactly pleasant
To see a beautiful setter on East Fifty-seventh Street looking
    for a woodcock or a pheasant.

German shepherds are useful for leading the blind,
And for biting burglars and Consolidated Edison men in the
    behind.

Lots of people have a rug.
Very few have a pug.

A Dog's Vigil
MARGARET E. BRUNER

There is a friendship that exists between
    So-called dumb animals; we often find
Them sorrowing with a grief that is as keen
    And deeply felt as those of humankind.

For many times this has been plainly shown
   To me, and yet more clearly when I read
The story of a dog who kept alone,
   A vigil when his mongrel pal lay dead.

Just how his pal met death I never knew—
   I know he kept a lonely watch all day,
Through bitter cold, and not until he grew
   Exhausted, would he let friends take away

The comrade he had known in happy hours;
   No human could have shown more faithfulness;
He could not tell his grief with words or flowers,
   But only with a puzzled, mute distress.

And when kind ones returned who bore away
   His lifeless friend, no watcher was in sight . . .
But travelers through a neighbor field, they say,
   Had seen a lonely dog pass by that night.

Dogs That Have Known Me
JEAN KERR

It's not just our own dogs that bother me. The dogs I meet at parties are even worse. I don't know what I've got that attracts them; it just doesn't bear thought. My husband swears I rub chopped meat on my ankles. But at every party it's the same thing. I am sitting in happy conviviality with a group in front of the fire when all of a sudden the large mutt of mine host appears in the archway. Then, without a single bark of warning, he hurls himself upon me. It always makes me think of that line from *A Streetcar Named Desire*—"Baby, we've had this date right from the beginning." My martini flies into space and my stockings are torn before he finally settles down peacefully in the lap of my new black faille. I blow out such quantities of hair as I haven't swallowed and glance at my host, expecting to be rescued. He murmurs, "Isn't that wonderful? You know, Brucie is usually so distant with strangers."

At a dinner party in Long Island last week, after I had been mugged by a large sheep dog, I announced quite piteously, "Oh dear, he seems to have swallowed one of my earrings." The hostess looked really distressed for a moment, until she examined the remaining earring. Then she said, "Oh, I think it will be all right. It's small and it's round."

Acknowledgments

The editors wish to thank the following for permission to reprint copyrighted material:

"Gulliver the Great" from *Gulliver the Great and Other Dog Stories*, copyright © 1916 by Walter A. Dyer, reprinted by permission of E. P. Dutton, a division of NAL Penguin, Inc.

"Sunning" from *Cricket, Cricket! The Best Loved Poems of James S. Tippett*; originally published in *A World To Know* by James S. Tippett, copyright © 1933 by Harper & Row, Publishers, Inc., reprinted by permission of Harper & Row, Publishers, Inc.

"The Dog of Pompeii" from *The Donkey of God* by Louis Untermeyer, copyright © 1932 by Harcourt Brace Jovanovich Inc., reprinted by permission of Harcourt Brace Jovanovich Inc.

"Sympathetic" from *Youngsters* by Burges Johnson, copyright 1921 by E. P. Dutton, renewed © 1949 by Burges Johnson, reprinted by permission of E. P. Dutton, a division of NAL Penguin Inc.

"pete at the seashore," "pete's holiday," and "confession of a glutton" from *the lives and times of archy and mehitabel* by Don Marquis, copyright © 1927 by Doubleday, a division of Bantam, Doubleday, Dell Publishing Group, Inc., reprinted by permission of the publisher.

"A Poem for Little Dogs" from *Silver Saturday*, copyright © 1937 by Nancy Byrd Turner, reprinted by permission of Dodd, Mead & Company.

"How the Friendship Grew" from *The Treasury of Dogs* by Arthur F. Jones and John Rendel, copyright © 1964 by Western Publishing Co., Inc., reprinted by permission of the publisher.

"The Power of the Dog" from *Actions and Reactions* by Rudyard Kipling, reprinted by permission of Doubleday, a division of Bantam, Doubleday, Dell Publishing Group, Inc.

"Snapshot of a Dog" from *The Middle-Aged Man on the Flying Trapeze* by James Thurber, copyright 1935 by James Thurber, renewed © 1963 by Helen Thurber and Rosemary A. Thurber, published by Harper & Row, Publishers, Inc. "The Thin Red Leash" from *Thurber's Dogs*, copyright 1955 by James Thurber, renewed © 1983 by Helen Thurber and Rosemary A. Thurber, published by Simon & Schuster, Inc. "A Dog's Lot" from the Introduction to *The Fireside Book of Dog Stories*, copyright 1943 by James Thurber, renewed © 1971 by Helen Thurber and Rosemary A. Thurber, published by Simon & Schuster, Inc. "Memorial" from *My World—and Welcome to It*, copyright 1943 by James Thurber, renewed 1970 by Helen Thurber and Rosemary A. Thurber, published by Harcourt Brace Jovanovich Inc. All Thurber selections reprinted by kind permission of Rosemary A. Thurber.

"The Dogs in My Life," "Gutsy," "The Dog Show: Heaven Help Us," and "Their Absolute All" from *A Celebration of Dogs*, copyright © 1982, 1984 by Roger Caras, reprinted by permission of Times Books, a division of Random House, Inc.

"The Dachshund" by John E. Donovan, from *The Saturday Evening Post*, reprinted by permission of The Curtis Publishing Company.

"Keeper—Emily Brontë's Boxer" from *Dogs of Destiny*, copyright © 1948 by Fairfax Downey, reprinted by permission of John Hawkins & Associates, Inc.

"Judy the Nurse Dog" from *James Herriot's Dog Stories*, copyright © 1986 by James Herriot, reprinted by permission of St. Martin's Press, Inc. and Harold Ober Associates, Inc.

"Little Lost Pup" from *Death and General Putnam* by Arthur Guiterman, reprinted by permission of Louise H. Sclove.

"Get Lost Buster, I'm in Charge Here" and "Living With People" from *Games Pets Play*, copyright © 1986 by Bruce Fogle, reprinted by permission of Viking Penguin Inc.

Acknowledgments

"The Care and Training of a Dog" from *One Man's Meat*, copyright © 1941 by E. B. White, originally appeared in *Harper's* Magazine, reprinted by permission of Harper & Row, Publishers, Inc. "Obituary," copyright 1932, renewed © 1960 by E. B. White, originally appeared in *The New Yorker*, reprinted by permission of the Estate of E. B. White. "Fashions In Dogs" from *The Fox of Peapack and Other Poems*, copyright © 1936 by E. B. White, originally appeared in *The New Yorker*, reprinted by permission of Harper & Row, Publishers, Inc.

"Dog Wanted" and "Dog In Chair" by Margaret Mackprang Mackay, from *The Saturday Evening Post*, reprinted by permission of The Curtis Publishing Co.

"Lone Dog" from *Songs to Save a Soul*, copyright © 1915 by Irene Rutherford McLeod, reprinted by permission of Viking Penguin Inc.

"Verse for a Certain Dog" from *The Portable Dorothy Parker*, copyright 1928, renewed © 1956 by Dorothy Parker, reprinted by permission of Viking Penguin Inc.

"Rx: One Loving Animal" from *Betty White's Pet Love* by Betty White with Thomas J. Watson, reprinted by permission of William Morrow & Co. Inc.

"The Hairy Dog" from *Pillicock Hill* by Herbert Asquith, reprinted by permission of Macmillan Publishing Co.

"My Dog" from *Rhymes About Ourselves* by Marchette Chute, originally published in 1943 by Macmillan Publishing Co., reprinted by permission of Elizabeth M. Roach.

"Blemie's Will" by Eugene O'Neill, reprinted by permission of The Yale Collection of American Literature, The Beinecke Rare Book and Manuscript Library, Yale University.

"The Animal with a Conscience" from *Man Meets Dog* by Konrad Lorenz, copyright 1953 by Konrad Lorenz, Marjorie Kerr, and Annie Eisenmenger, reprinted by permission of Houghton Mifflin Co. and the author.

"The Dog" from *Custard and Company*, copyright 1957 by Ogden Nash, renewed © 1985 by Frances Nash, Isabel Nash Eberstadt, and Linnell Nash Smith. "An Introduction to Dogs" from *The Face Is Familiar*, copyright © 1936 by Ogden Nash, first published in the *New York American*. Both selections reprinted by permission of Little, Brown & Co.

"Lost Dog" by Frances Rodman, from *The New York Times*, March 28, 1932. "To A Dog, Grown Blind" by Mazie V. Caruthers, from *The New York Times*, April 23, 1940. Both selections reprinted by permission of *The New York Times*.

"To My Dog" by John Galsworthy, from *The Collected Poems of John Galsworthy*, copyright 1934, renewed © 1962 by Charles Scribner's Sons, reprinted by permission of Charles Scribner's Sons, an imprint of Macmillan Publishing Co.

"Sleeping Habits of the Neurotic Dog" and "What Makes the Dog Neurotic?" from *How to Live with a Neurotic Dog* by Stephen Baker, copyright © 1960 by Prentice Hall, reprinted by permission of the author.

"A Prayer for Dogs" by Goldie C. Smith, from *The Saturday Evening Post*, reprinted by permission of The Curtis Publishing Co.

"Mongrel Type Dog" from *Dogs*, copyright © 1976 by Henry Morgan and George Booth, reprinted by permission of Houghton Mifflin Co.

"The Dog Who Paid Cash" from *Autobiography of Will Rogers*, edited by Donald Day, copyright 1949 by Rogers Company, renewed © 1977 by Donald Day and Beth Day, reprinted by permission of Houghton Mifflin Co.

"The Outlaw" by Robert W. Service, copyright © 1916 by Dodd, Mead & Co., reprinted by permission of Dodd, Mead & Co. and the Estate of Robert W. Service.

"Dogs That Have Known Me" from *Please Don't Eat the Daisies* by Jean Kerr, copyright © 1957 by Conde Nast Publications, Inc., reprinted by permission of Doubleday, a division of Bantam, Doubleday, Dell Publishing Group, Inc.

Works by the following authors appear without permission, as best efforts to locate the copyright holders were unsuccessful:
Berton Braley, Milly Walton, Marty Hale, Alexander Woollcott, Hugh Walpole, Leroy J. Fleury, Richard Joseph, Mrs. E. Worthing, Douglas Malloch, W. L. Mason, Teddy Webb, Helen Welshimer, Arthur Wallace Peach, William Hankins Chitwood, Peg Roland, Albert Payson Terhune, Ralph Wotherspoon, Hallie Carrington Brent, Margaret E. Bruner, June Provine, Isla Paschal Richardson, Esther Birdsall Darling, A. C. Gate, Inez Clark Thorson.